Treasures of the Creative Spirit

FOR JANE AND
THE TREASURE OF
HER SPIRIT!

WARMLY,

R. Peikenberg

Treasures of the Creative Spirit

An Artist's Understanding of Human Creativity

Robert Piepenburg

PEBBLE PRESS INC.
MICHIGAN

To your spirit and creative future . . .

Pebble Press Inc.
24723 Westmoreland
Farmington Hills, MI 48336-1963

Publisher's Cataloging in Publication Data
Treasures of the creative spirit / Robert Piepenburg.—1st ed.
1. Life—Spiritual life. 2. Creation (Artistic)—Inspiration, motivation,
etc.   3. Self-perception - Self-awareness.   4. Self-realization in art.

ISBN: 0-9628481-3-1

Library of Congress Catalog Card Number: 97-075980

Cover drawing by Gail Piepenburg
Printed in the United States of America

Contents

Introduction

There are mysterious connections between creativity and spirituality that shape existence and contribute to our evolution. This book is about those connections. Much in the same way that some questions can have several right answers or some answers several essential explanations, a creative response to a specific need can take many forms. If, however, a response lacks a mindful sense of self; has no spirit to pal with, it is less likely to find a new place in the world or, more importantly, a joyful place within one's self.

As human beings we are visionaries filled with imagination. We are also intimately blessed with the subjective presence of our spirit and our spirit, like the eye of a hurricane, is the inner eye of self. This, then, is a book about our spiritual treasures and how they form the functioning bridges between our being human and our being creative. It is about our capacity to be creative and to give expression to our imagination even when the details of its existence are unknown to us. It is a guide that takes us spinning and turning through the senses, to the human realities of being creative, and ultimately to the identity center of our being.

Robert Piepenburg
Captiva Island, Florida

I

SPIRIT AND CREATIVITY

1

A Connection to Connections

W hat is the expression of spirit, if not the ultimate description for creativity?

Creativity is the reality presence of spirit. As a transmission of spirit, creativity is a primal transcendent force. It gives birth to form; to new entities. Without its emergence we are without the means to issue forth anything else. Without its universal presence we would be unable to conceptualize—new thinking would not unfold, living would not advance and matter would not change.

Evolution itself is an all-inclusive creative process. As a majestic series of simultaneous transformations, it continuously goes beyond everything that has already occurred. Not only is this transforming emergence a natural part of the cosmos, it is a profound human capacity of infinite and extraordinary possibilities.

Human beings are forever evolving in a comprehensive array of external and internal ways. Creative experiences that take the highest states of human consciousness into account, while at times appearing deceptively simple, are manifestations of the spirit: that knowing voice of personal truth that we quietly honor and hold sacred deep within us.

The spirit initiates change, produces change and dignifies change. It is an intangible aspect of existence. Still, there is little within the domain of human activity that isn't touched, directed or consecrated by it. In various mind-boggling forms, it is the supreme self-expanding power. Yet part of what is so incredible about this whole process, is that it is often only within the process itself, that different visions of spirit are found.

As is a personal feeling of being, our spirit is a perception as intimate as breath itself. Creativity, in the service of spirituality, is simply an affirmation of beingness. Such creative affirmations, to be sure, have their universal qualities (much in the same way that love, everywhere, is accompanied by hope) but such connections are always more important to the individual doing the work than they are to those witnessing it.

Art, like creativity, is also an affirmation of spirit. And even though it too may have a universe of spectators it is the expression of the artist's spirit, not the viewers, that gives shape and value to works of art. Later, the spirit of the viewer may identify or find inspiration in the work and reinforce its value but such findings are of little importance compared to the concerns of the artist. Creative activity can result in greatness but that seldom, if ever, has anything to do with the personal work of being and becoming more in touch with who one is. For the artist, fame and fortune notwithstanding, it is important that the art be a direct response to the inspirational gifts of their spirit and that they be gifted in return with a new vision of self.

Through the dynamics of this spiritual give-and-take the artist initiates an autobiographical truthfulness resulting in art that is embraced as "their work". The art, "their work", may end up being wonderfully creative gifts to humanity but first and foremost it is a gift to themselves. Creativity is always a spiritual immersion into self and it is empowered whenever one's sense of self is united with the reality of their life through the communion of their spirit.

This book was not written to make you into an artist but to make you aware of the spirit living within you— your greatest treasure. Whether we know it as love, freedom, hope, trust or by other titles, it is what allows us to live creative lives—an awareness of which being an artist depends upon.

Your spirit is never absent from your life. As you experience it, you experience yourself. Experience is a name we give to life. Through it, we are united with our awareness of self. Such a transformation expands our capacity to be creative. Experience is the teacher that gives us lessons on how to live more creatively . . . even if we're not listening. Our creativeness is real. It exists. It is a natural part of our being. When a person is not living creatively it means that they are not being aware of who they are; that they are not remaining in touch with their spirit.

While I have just embraced the connections between spirit and creativity through the experience of being an artist this in no way means to imply that the moments and activities of creative living that each of us generates daily, as we go about doing our work and caring for our homes and families, is any less spirit-filled or less important than the lasting work of extraordinary artists. It simply means that this is one way to come to creative consciousness. My experience in my work is that of an artist. Art and artists are preeminent examples of creativity and creative individuals, which is why they are frequently referenced, but again please remember that one does not have to be artistic to be creative. Creativity is every bit about valuing and being open to the wonders of life as it is about expressing those experiences.

To be creative one doesn't have to be original. No one creates in a vacuum, through and by themselves. Being creative, as many artists know, is simply participating in the ongoing realities of life. Life is an eternal form of creation and when we give expression to our life we are, in a spiritual sense, being creative. And, when that expression is given permanence we are, in a creative sense, being artistic.

There are many, many ways to approach human creativity. It could be looked at culturally, socially, historically or even mythically as there are many inseparable forces that play fundamental roles in the spirit's unfolding. If I were a Freudian psychologist, for example, I might choose to examine the human spirit with reference to the ego or sexuality. If I were a theologian I might look at things in a religious context or what has been called the organizational worship of spirituality. If I were a mystic, perhaps in an awe inspiring transpersonal context. If I were a Buddhist I would have an even different interpretation, but my spirit energy was awakened as an artist and flows most expressively in an art context.

My aspiring quest for comprehension existed in an art scenario that was equally filled with courage and passion. Alive to my own creative sources, some more obvious than others, I have come to deeply care about the corresponding connections between spirit and creativity and share their capacities with you, as an artist, not that you might go bravely forward to create brilliant works of art but so that you can release those pent-up, self-limiting needs that seemed beyond your reach, maybe even in childhood, and bring more passion and creativity to whatever you do today as an adult.

Consider this. The wisdom of the spirit respects the creative power within you. And, once this connection is understood as a profound affirmation of self, the expression of your creative uniqueness honors the depth of your spirit.

Creative activity is fertile ground on which to greet, interact and to bond with the various aspects of spiritual wisdom. As a place of sanctification, it is where the spirit is most often anointed. It is where, within a human context of emergent creativeness, the important connections are made. Connections that help us to see how the truths of our being have value and how they correspond with known realities, be they externally objective, culturally collective or internally subjective.

By discovering these evolving connections to our creativity we are less likely to apply life's energy in unimaginative ways and in the wrong places. Or, to use studio imagery, less likely to apply paint on the easel instead of the canvas. Through the conscious recognition of each other, a new and affectionate life line between self and spirit is realized. Mature connections abound and one becomes silently born to live creatively on a canvas of new possibilities.

In being creative we honor our existence and the gifts of our spirit. While the teacher in me is tempted to call these gifts *life-skills*, the artist in me wants to view them as pigments: as a painter's palette with a full range of color from which to render life to all of one's visions. Our creativity is ongrowing. Each time we pick up the brush we give added praise to our spirit and whenever we paint from our palette we give color to our identity.

To connect with your own creative sources (your spirit resources) is a liberating achievement. The day that you come to trust in your own personal truth is not just another "lucky" day, it is the day you embrace your creativity and gain a clearer understanding of your tommorows. It is a day of release, from a limited to a higher order of sensibility, not as much a consciousness of celebration as a celebration of consciousness.

2

Spirituality: The Stem Of Life

Spirit is the essence of the natural self. It is the passion that directs our life. It is the supporting stalk—the connecting trunk to every leaf and to every flower that blooms. It is the real source of all of our creative possibilities.

The spirit, as a maternal cradle in which images of self are initially cared for, is wholesome, consummate, innocent and divine.

As important as the spirit is to one's life, there are a multiplicity of intangible elements that claim influence and mutual loyalty for the integration of their contributions to enlightenment. The soul, heart and mind each have valid, yet different, dimensions of awareness to offer and need to be interpreted within the context in which they are situated.

A common misinterpretation, for example, is one that confuses soul with an understanding of subjective truthfulness, and equates it with the spirit. Spirit is life and life is spirit, but life is not soul. While not easy, the trick to recognizing correlations between spirit, soul, heart and mind involves some subjective hair splitting. You must decide!

The soul, as the disguised carrier of karmic memory, is the consciousness of the spirit. Without flexing muscles, it stirs, prods and, drawing on intimate experience, initiates the spirit to what's transpired. Tied to history, it enriches the influences, virtues and failures of the past with the redeemable qualities of the present. And, while the soul may hold the transcended knowledge of life's experiences it is the spirit that actually carries that attainment into the ever-expanding passages of a person's life.

The heart, as the wise counselor of inner vision, is the compassionate navigator of the spirit. The blessings of its beloved insights are often beyond our self-imagination, yet nothing is beyond its wisdom. The spirit delights in interacting with the special nuances of the love-embedded heart, so much so, that spiritual enlightenment is always a reflection of engagements with it.

The mind, as a practical sentry of objectivity, is the judgmental modifier of the spirit. At times we are tempted to rely upon the mind as a conclusive source of information pertaining to the dynamics of our individual potential, when in actuality it is often the mind that imposes limits in life and resists our creativity. Often we hear the phrase "The sky's the limit!" In an idealized way the mind can rationally imagine this to be so, but it is the spirit that undertakes the efforts to embrace the universe and give unity to life.

Thus, our spirit is not our mind and certainly not our body, even though it knows these and other aspects of our being. Spirit is an invisible yet infinite force, a freedom, a power, a cosmic wisdom—a you name it—that seemingly flows through us and that has the potential to spontaneously enrich our understanding, expand perception, extend life, generate creative action or any number of human achievements and still leave us with no rational way to explain or define its reality. Our spirit is forever an available and blessed part of our being but, for many of our self and life imposed circumstances, often remains hidden from us. Fortunately, however, it is possible (as were many things that we might have once thought impossible) to open our personal shutters to the light of spirit consciousness and to discover a joy-filled life of creative potential.

Spirit consciousness is the highest creative achievement. It is the ultimate creative emergence. It is truth. It is love. It is all things in their purist form.

To experience the spiritual awareness of this divine state is to experience a oneness with life itself. Without exceptions, creative activities that occur while in this state possess a genius or magical power that is seldom attainable at other levels of consciousness, save for those occurring during the innocence of young childhood.

As children we come from a nativity of creativity. Our emergence from the womb is our first creative achievement, and everyday thereafter we perform one creative miracle after another as we grow into the unlimited possibilities of our life. Those early days of uncorrupted creativity do not, however, last for long before our behavior begins to become tainted by ego and identity development. As our self-image evolves, it does so in ways that often disown important aspects of our true selves and it is only much later in life, after we acquire both the wisdom to know (to see) and the virtue to do (to be), that we are able to return to quality places where the purity of our essence once again is a reflection of unbounded creativeness. Places of primal prominence, where the imagination is again both welcomed and nurtured within a special coexistence with life.

Child psychologists have identified a number of pre-adolescent needs and recognized a number of generic adolescent behavior patterns. Children, even during their early years, unconsciously want to know "Who am I ?" and "Why am I here ?", questions that we consciously and frequently ask ourselves as adults in our instinctual hunger for meaningfulness. Childhood needs all too soon become self-image needs: compelling needs of the mind rather than those of the spirit. It is said, for example, that what we desire and experience is an experience of our own consciousness. In other words, our thinking mirrors our perceptions; reflects our hopeful fantasies. When young, we my have various unconditional needs, needs that entangle us in consequences, but fortunately the dynamics of living continuously moves us forward, toward revelation, irregardless of our impoverished will.

As we transform from childhood into adolescence, youth, adulthood and maturity we outgrow self-image needs, or any number of other self sacrificing needs, and experience a self-reliant emergence with an ever expanding awareness of life. We ascend to a higher consciousness and grow into our spirituality. Spirituality, in this sense, is the ascendance of the spirit to a place of wholeness where all of life is both seen and felt as being a sensory part of one's self.

By separating ourselves from unnecessary desires for image enhancement we may free up enough of our image maintenance/projection energy to actually get a look at ourselves not as a self who is seeking or needing acceptance but as a self that is empowered with an energy of spirit, an energy of love.

Our spirituality is not a symptom or a shadow of self, it is the subjective "truth" of self. It is neither manufactured or forced. When we create in spirit consciousness, we create for the pure, pleasing joy of creating. We do not create for money, power or things transient. When the spirit is in awakened attendance, passion and compassion are manifested, and we are transformed into a more creative version of who we once were.

Creation is inseparable from spirit. Both are vital life forces; each essential to the unfolding of our humanness. But when spirit is present, creation does not remain as object—as an "it": an external entity lacking human qualification and virtue. With spirit, creation becomes subjective. The spiritual element is what infuses object creation with meaningfulness . . . with an interlocking of human depth. Without a spiritual presence life's creations may posses functional applications yet remain endlessly dull, with no holistic goodness or sublime virtuousness—no majesty! Figuratively, they would be lacking in color, sound, smell and texture. They would not be revealing of our true nature, they would not mirror the truth of our existence or connect us with the mystery of our own lives. As I see it, every thought, act and object becomes a creative work when it radiates with our human spirituality and reveals a relationship with the beauty of our life.

John Ruskin has said that great men have a ". . . feeling that greatness is not in them, but through them". Likewise, spirituality can keenly be felt as something that flows through us. As an overwhelming force it carries the human elements of genesis.

Our spirit desires recognition and requires attention. Part of its nature is to be of creative use. The spirit, however, is not stitched to our body. It can leave us from time-to-time, making our task of keeping watch over it that much more important.

Creative functioning is impaired by a loss of spirit energy. This also holds true for one's emotional, social and physical well-being. Our spirit isn't always with us. And, due to a lack of care or even acknowledgment, it may barely be alive even when it is with us. Whenever the spirit is suppressed or denied care our entire existence suffers because it is just not the core of our internal life but of our external life as well. Although there are strong gravitational-like pulls on our interior lives from many external forces, we have a primordial motivation to claim and keep hold of our spirit. And, when seemingly lost, a natural need to recover it.

Our spirit has so many services to perform in relationship to our wholeness that it is multi-functional. It is, in an operational sense, the bones of our character and the marrow of our wisdom. To keep it intact requires masterful flexibility and to keep it alive requires responsibility. Spirituality thrives on attitude: on how we choose to respond to the circumstances surrounding our life. When Eleanor Roosevelt said "No one can make you feel inferior without your consent" she could just as easily have substituted the word "dispirited" for the word "inferior". A positive reaction to the ordinary and not so ordinary experiences in life is an inner power that we have the freedom of choosing. By remaining conscious of the responsibility we have for maintaining our inner environment—our being—we are more able to provide for the all important treasurers of the spirit. In so doing, we invite the blossoming of our own spirituality and an openness to the simple wonder of our imagination.

3

Creativity: Petals of the Blossom

Creativity, in its most unencumbered and universal form, is astonishingly spiritual when it is an expression of love and honors our own humanity. Like a flower, it is most beautiful when in full bloom and the rich colors of the petals open us to our own joy and awaken us, once again, to the mysteries of life. The great yet simple role that each petal plays in the ripening and overall beauty of the flower is much like the role that each treasure of the spirit plays in the nurturing of a creative life.

It is true that no two flowers are or look the same just as no two people are the same; personally, physically or creatively. But just as there are many petals to a flower there are many components to creativity.

All of human growth, discovery and advancement embodies human creativity.

Creativity itself is not a qualifiable thing or entity. In many respects it may not even be a process or a causation. Ultimately, it is simply the path to a greater awakening. It is not a manifest end, but rather a supportive base for the ascension of our capacities to go to a higher place. Maybe even to the Divine itself.

There are those who affirm that when we're actively being creative we are, in a very God-like sense, participating in the eternal continuation of the ultimate creative act, that of Creation itself: that beginning point of time—the beginning of history.

The painter Barnett Newman felt that art was more than form, color and composition; that its content was a probe into mystery . . . not into the personality of the artist, but rather into that of the world's. For Newman, being creative was discovering the truth of creation. To him, being creative was being an artist both for and with the Divine Creator in that he too, sought to bring forth truth from chaos: the void of the unknown.

The original act of creation, that the Divine Creator put into motion when creating the world and all of its inhabitants, has allowed each of us to become our own world unto our selves. In other words, every advance we have made toward our own becoming—toward the wholeness of our being—has been a creative achievement of great personal value and an evolutionary continuation of that first radiant act.

Perhaps you have heard the following words from a song that goes something like this: *"Put a little clay . . . on the potter's wheel . . . give it a spin . . . know how God must feel."* Creativity as nirvana, as an experience characterized by states of reincarnations or reunion, well maybe, but there are other more direct and identifiable ways of embracing it. According to the non-canonical Gospel of Thomas, for example, *That which you bring forth from within yourself will save you. That which you do not bring forth from within will destroy you.* Creativity is a life necessity. It's at the center of all great achievements and it is also a way in which we can find ourselves, our center. Without this transforming force there is no continuity of wholeness in life; of self. Without creation consciousness, our life, and its many paths, will seldom inspire us to partake of its fullness. Our womb birth was a creative miracle, yet it is only the first of many acts of creation the self will live through. Self-creation is an unending expression of creation consciousness.

When we're being creative we often use our body in physical ways to transform our surroundings and re-compose our life, yet the body is not the creative force.

29

All such physical activity is (creatively speaking) neutral. In such instances, the body is only a divisive servant of the spirit—a much greater and higher force of extraordinary possibilities—and solely responds to its directions. Again, referring to the Gospel of Thomas, we read *Woe to the soul that depends on the flesh.*

Our bodies are essential to our creative functioning but the centering force for that behavior is inherently personal. In other words, personal perception directs creative behavior and our life becomes a canvas for the colors of our enlightenment. Once this essential truth is understood, once creativity is beheld as a sensory union to our perceptions and imagination, it becomes quite simple to locate the real origins of its nativity and to live a richer life. Of course, discovering the sources of your creative identity and knowing how to gracefully bring it forth without limitations are two separate issues. This latter and somewhat more complex issue of self transcendence and the emergence of our creative being is what the final section of this book is committed to exploring and empowering.

Creativity is a natural way of bringing forth the spirit of our love and extending it to others. Spirit, in this context, is the invisible love that dwells inside us and creativity, in its deepest form, is the visible expression of that love. Creative vision could not occur without love. Love is what sensitizes and focuses the spirit. In its purest and most complete form it gives purpose to most of what we do. And, unlike worldly wealth or power, it provides the ultimate value to everything we do in our everyday life. To live more creatively one only needs to recognize the importance of one's spirit and to look within for love's guidance. Through such an orientation to living one can become not only a thoroughly creative person but a loving one as well.

As a universal force, love fertilizes the seeds of creation and inspires an intrinsic motivation to create. Every individual possesses a different mix of physical, mental and social skills, but none of these unique talents are of much creative value until they converge with an individual's intrinsic interests. Intrinsic interests are those that are kindled internally and allowed to flourish externally. They are the forces from within that move us to do things we find to be personally enjoyable, satisfying or even challenging. These things, these activities, are primarily undertaken for their own sake and not necessarily for external recognition or rewards. What occurs inevitably, of course, is that self-motivation evolves into self-determination and when this powerful combination of forces, call it desire, drive, dedication or even obsession, crisscrosses with one's natural or endowed abilities the potential for creative action is dramatically increased.

In life, creativity and spirituality are partners. They

are like the two sides of a coin; where you find one, you'll always find the other. What is unfortunate, however, is that some people never fully realize either one of them. For to do so, one must first acknowledge their existence. Which in itself is no easy accomplishment being that they are, by nature, metaphysical—an elusive reality that is somewhat speculative and mystical. More subjective than objective. Second, one needs to yield before them: to courteously give way to their authority.

Even though our creativity and spirituality are an intimate part of our existence they still need to be consciously acknowledged and accepted as primal agents of our identity. By accepting them we bring them forth and they become easier to live with in our objectified world. Its possible to possess a knowledge of our creativity and a faith in our spirit but still be unable to express ourselves in meaningful ways.

So what then does being creative entail? Being creative in this sense is going beyond the point of self-realization and into the knowing spirit energy of *self.* In a humble sense it is the replacement of a personal self with a universal self somewhat similar to that age-old adage that " . . . one must first lose one's self to find one's self." In an even bigger sense, it is a yielding acceptance of our spiritual heritage. Which is, ultimately, the independence of the *self* to be free and to blossom in that freedom. If you understand this, you'll know what I mean when I say that works of art are not made with materials, but with the spirit of *self*.

There's an all too common myth about creativity: that it is solely the domain of artists. Its true that music, writing, sculpture or acting can be dramatic pinnacles of creative expression; but creativity, as a genuine expression of *self*, is in no way limited to the arts. Creativity, as a flexible omnifarious of thoughts, feelings, values or any number of those unique treasures that comprise our spirit, is an infinitely personal means for reshaping both the internal and external dimensions of our life. Of course, creativity is many things. But there is one certainty—it expresses who we are: it is being our real self.

4

Teaching and Learning

Teaching and learning are a foundational part of everything we do in life. They lead us to all things, becoming an expansive roadway between spirit and self. It is on this organic road that creativity comes our way.

As a human being, and also as a teacher, artist, husband, father, friend, etc., my life is profoundly based upon the gifts of the spirit. At times I may place more weight on one area than another. Take the area of *integrity*, for example. There are times when that one single spiritual gift or concept guides my entire life. If, as a teacher, I bring the transforming power of just this one graceful virtue to the relationship I have with students, with my colleagues, with my subject matter, with my college, with my community, etc., then I have an enormous opportunity to help the flowers of creativity bloom.

If, at the same time, I let everything I do as a teacher also be based upon *love,* can you imagine how the spirit is opened even wider and how a new dawning of light can be brought to shine on the internal landscape of others? When a student feels a genuine extension of a teacher's integrity and a teacher's love towards them they cannot help but perceive it as a purifying breeze that moves them closer to their creative life force; connecting them with the heart of their interests. And, if my teaching was also based upon the concept of *freedom,* can you imagine, again, how my respect for just this gift alone would simultaneously uncover fears, foster creativity and hold students in fulfillment?

On the other hand, if teaching were not based upon some sense of the spiritual in everyday living, but rather on external factors, students would experience little in the way of creative understanding and achievement. There are teachers who are demanding tyrants, disciplinarians, controllers who judgmentally make all of the decisions for their students, who chip away at student esteem to ease their own despair, who give endless lectures of emptiness-without feeling. As with every act of control, they weaken their capacity to bring out the best in themselves and, ultimately, in others.

Creativity, like a flower, is richly delicate. It thrives with nourishment and wilts with neglect. As a fragile integration of invited awareness and unexpected possibilities, creativity is an amplification of experience; a journey to a new and more trusted identity. If you're in a creative quest and seek guidance in the form of a teacher, seek those who provide you with an environment that is both empty of any limitations to your spirit and filled with the compassion of their own spirit. If anything, good teaching has the responsibility to bring the human spirit into creative activity. And, a creative teacher brings forth the creative strengths of their students through the very nature of their own creative activity. The depth of a teacher's creative spirit is, moment-by-moment, an invaluable source of encouragement and inspiration for students. Invaluable in the sense that it teaches students how to find it within themselves and special in the sense that it affords them an opportunity to learn the virtues of being truthful and honest with themselves.

Learning is many things. It is a quest for understanding, an attempt to find new perspectives from which to understand the human condition as well as the dimensions of our own nature. Creatively, learning is also an orientation process. It is identified as the information integrator for all subsequent creative activity. Creativity, like learning, instigates a changing of perceptions. It is a breaking away from the past, a confinement of the old, and a corridor of freedom to the present. Whenever we alter our perceptions, and leave the past behind, we are alive in the present and creating our future. With every new perception life is made new.

When we're learning and being creative we are actively choosing to give birth to a greater expression of self. To a larger reality. Our creativity is our resurrection and it is one of life's dramas that we will continue to reenact . . . only never in the same way twice.

If we view creativity as a less than significant aspect of our life, then it will be insignificant to us, but if we hold it dear to our heart, and bring its energy to our spirit, then we will be blessed by its presence. A creative spirit, like a good teacher, opens new pathways and guides our steps to what is possible. Our creativity increases our capacity for discovering a genuine independence that will remain within us and allow us to go forth in life with the trust and the freedom to live life fully.

"A cheerful heart is good medicine, but a crushed spirit dries up the bones" (Proverbs 17:22). Whenever life lacks creative union or loses significance you can bet its lacking in love of spirit. Many people believe that we're creative because of love. Yes, love is a potent force but, in reality, our creativeness is a manifestation of our love of spirit. Our spirit is what we create with. Our spirit is what empowers love and vice versa. Our spirit is not only our hope in life, it is our life.

If you teach you perform a sacred duty and just as one teaches with spirit one learns with spirit. In one sense learning is the pioneering transcendence of a non-spirited self to a spirited self. Learning is an ascension to a sacredness of being that can lead to an integrated completion of self.

It seems that every semester I have conversations with art students who express a deep personal fear in their ability to be creative that results from some ongoing struggle within themselves, some self-inflicted feelings of worthlessness that causes them to respond to life for its capacity to distract them rather than to engage them. A big part of being creative is staying focused on who one is rather than on what one is. It is the difference between spirit *self* and ego *self.* By using the ego here to symbolically reference external forces and the spirit internal forces we can have a clearer picture of how one can be considered creative. Because our internal world is our real truth, external truths often become overstated as a means of atonement and one way that our external life attempts to neutralize our spirit life is by projecting images of hard work where one has to over-achieve in some perfectionist way to be anywhere close to being

39

creative when in fact it seeks to choke off creative confidence.

As many artists know, creativity cannot be regulated judiciously. If it's going to occur naturally and honestly, the ego of the *self* will have to submit to the spirit of the *self*. Such is the wisdom of awareness and the power of surrendering.

The creative awareness and intelligence of the dancer is seen in the body but resides in the spirit. The potter's hands touch the clay but spirit is what gives it shape. Musically, the singer and not the song is what makes the difference: the singer is spirit. The spirit is the genuine energy of *self*. It is the muscle of activity; the passion of art. And our ability to respond to this deep source of creation consciousness, a resource far more profound than the mind, is what validates our actions; literally rendering them as true creative extensions of who we are.

What those students didn't yet know when they expressed doubts in their own creative capabilities was that being creative is about knowing who you are before its about being what you accomplish.

Literally, we physically survive by acknowledging our real selves and by creatively giving form to that personal acceptance. As spiritual beings we are independently free to identify the real needs of our existence and gifted with a great energy to creatively meet those needs in fresh new ways that can be exquisitely positive and totally affirmative. The more I, as a human being and as a teacher, accept and act on this gift, this treasure of my spirit, the more balanced my life becomes and the more able I am to mirror this peaceful form of knowledge to a student who has not yet taken their happiness in it. And, just as happiness seeks happiness, balance begets balance until it sustains a personal inner calm that both supports and generates creative responses to one's self, and the world at large, that are seemingly effortless.

5

The Hero Within

Often I've answered questions relating to creativity and how one might go about finding a more creative solution to a particular problem, but yesterday, for the first time, I was actually asked how one can become creative. This was a very simple yet direct question, "How does someone become creative?" My answer was quickly given and, if you've just read the last couple of pages, contained no surprises. I simply replied that all one had to do was to acknowledge the fact that they were already creative and to submit to it.

Yes, it is a fact, we are all born as creative beings. It is a natural part of our heritage: our humanness. In knowing and accepting this, all that is left to do is to acquiesce. Yes, give way, cease the struggle, throw in the towel. Resign yourself to fact that you are creative . . . grin and "creatively" bear it!

So, you might ask, "If we're so endowed how is it that I struggle so much at being creative and why does it so often elude me?" The main reason I believe why so many feel as if its missing in their life, is that inside they just don't feel creative.

Insecurity subverts creativity. Perhaps the important question to ask in such instances is "Whose definition of creativity am I using?" If, for example, someone is having difficulty with being self-assertive or with challenging the status quo they are not acting on their own creative insights or honoring their creative self. If, on the other hand, that same person were to be honest with themself and recognize that their present behavior standards were not really their own, they would feel freer and their potential for creative living would immediately improve.

Being creative is being honest about who you are. Self honesty is the prerequisite to creative expression—to creative living. People who hide from themselves are unable to develop a clear understanding of their own values and therefor lack the beliefs to meet the greater challenges of their spirit. And the spirit, you must realize, is the real hero of the creative self.

As we grow into self knowledge, our honesty defines our values and as they assume a larger role in our identity they become gifts for our spirit. Our spirit, in turn, assimilates them. It welcomes them in and maintains them as standards for our own becoming. In its perfect keeping they take on a new importance . . . eventually becoming valued treasures of our spirit. When the time is right or the need strong our spirit gives them back to us as majestic gifts to be creatively used in the form of love, art or whatever good work we might want to commit our loyalties and passions too.

Creativity has no resistance. It is we who often resist it. We keep knocking on its door when all we really have to do is turn the knob to enter into it. As an artist, I have come to recognize both the place and the value of human spirituality in life. Unlike a mirror which only reflects one's image, creativity reflects one's spirit and one's spirit is more than one's creative nature, it is ones life. In life there is a rich range of feelings to be experienced and vital choices to be made. Whenever we find ourselves at a crossroads it is for each of us to unite with our spirit, make those choices, and move forward, hopefully, to flourish. Ultimately the choices are ours to make. We are the authors, the choreographers, the painters, the actors, etc. of our own existence. We create our life: our world. Creativity doesn't just enhance. It generates. It's about formation not just transformation.

The creative hero within each of us is more concerned about being authentic than about being original. It's how we make a more human and reverent sanctuary for our spirit.

Therapists love to take people into their past. True, we can learn a lot about ourselves by embracing our history, but the journey can become an prolonged exercise in distraction: an exhaustive debate. Just as the pedestal without the icon is useless, it may serve no real purpose. While we cannot undo any damaging events from our past, neither do we need to make the present its grave-yard. We can choose to live with self-doubt or we can choose to live with glory. Yes, its an action that requires courage and not defensiveness. Defensiveness substantially reduces possibilities, and artists are people moved by the discovery of choice. They live in its fullness and have respect for it as a creative force. This might be a time and a place to ask yourself what it is that moves you? But first, recognize this truth: a personal thought is just a personal thought until you choose to do something with it. How different, for example, would your world be today if people like Mozart, Michelangelo, Edison or your own mother hadn't chosen to give expression to their creative thoughts?

The freedom of choice and the choice of freedom reveal an equilibrium; an integration of awareness and behavior. In such a context the immortal Nike ad "JUST

DO IT" speaks of emancipation. It inspires us to be alive in the moment. Our present self is our real self. The "now" can be our time to take up the wings of spirit and, with a great sense of freedom, make creative flights in the skies of life. Julia Cameron, in her book *The Vein of Gold*, lists ten "survival rules" for artists. The first of which is *Acceptance.* Here, she too writes "Just do it." Warning us not to second-guess ourselve's and avoid the simple fact that we're already creatively capable of artistic expression.

We all search for outward expression while at the same time seeking some form of inner peace. We all have a desire to become more creatively expressive. If this is your goal, and if you also wish to achieve it within the context of you own spirituality, than the following section is for you—like a warm sunny field of spring flowers—to wander in. And, like the child who wanders through a flowering field and unexpectedly becomes wealthy, may you find a treasure of self-affirming riches.

II

TREASURES OF THE SPIRIT

6

Visions

Visions have an astounding power. They are the dreams that we live in when were being creative and forming the realities of our future. When shared, they influence others, direct events and attract circumstances. In 1501 Michelangelo had a vision for his sculpture of *David*, in 1516 Luther had a vision of religious reformation, in 1861 Lincoln had a vision of freedom, in 1930 Gandhi had a vision for non-violence, in 1964 King had a vision for equality. Lists of visionaries such as this are endless; every one can be found on one but not every vision, like a vision called Microsoft by Bill Gates, comes to fulfillment.

Visions are promises of possibilities. As the seeds of creative change, they need to be nurtured if they are to blossom and mature into realness. For a vision to be realized it must be perceived by the visualizer as truly desirable and worthy of achievement. Without a real commitment, the visionary is without the creative energies to influence circumstance and expand opportunities. Action and the continuation of action is what works here. To transform a vision, to bring it into existence, the spirit has to be strong to survive failures and seemingly insurmountable odds. It has to be brave to go forward into the darkness of the unexplored.

In both undergraduate and graduate school I was fortunate to have had some art instructors who understood the magical force of personal visions, intentions and desires. If I hadn't had such teachers, it would have taken much longer to realize that a vision precedes creative action, choreographs its every movement, and not the other way around. Still, I had a number of art teachers (persons whom you think would better understand the mechanics of creativity) who felt that techniques and procedures had to always come first. A feeling that one had to "have" before they could "be". Yes, the "how-to" part of art making is important, but not when it is mistaken for the art; not when it subverts creative insight. What happens with some teachers is that they become perfunctorily involved with construction details and never get around to honoring the work's source or purpose. Without a willingness to trust that methods can readily, and excitedly, be derived for actualizing visions they run the risk of permanently damaging the creative drive in students.

As an energizing force, visions carry forth creative consciousness and are the initial expressive links between our spirit and the world. They appear without words, sometimes without thinking, but they are a creative part of everything mankind has made and brought to our life. Throughout history the works of men and women have always taken new direction and shape when the dimensions of their human spirit and personal visions embraced one another.

George Eastman, who in the 1880's became known as the father of "popular" photography, was a man of great vision and generosity. Fascinated with photography but not with the cumbersome equipment and time-consuming processing of dry plate film, he advanced a vision for simplifying photographic processing by perfecting flexible film and creating a portable compact camera he named "Kodak". All, for the purpose of making picture taking available to everyone. George Eastman realized his vision—his ideal. With the press of a button all of us are now able to take those photographs that immortalize life's precious moments.

Each of us has choices to make in life, choices between loving and hating, creating and destroying and so on. One of the choices Eastman had to make was that of being either a giver or a taker. He and his vision took the side of giving. As his fortune grew he gave over 100 million dollars, anonymously whenever possible, to the community and a multitude of worthy causes. As an employer, he was among the first to provide extensive health care and retirement benefits to his employees. He was a rich man, not just in dollars but in spirit, for the dollars were given away while he was still living, and those that weren't, like all wealth, were given away upon his death. He is the kind of individual that is remembered for being rich in deed and in spirit and that type of recognition lasts forever.

Visions are our maps. "When there is no vision people perish." (Proverbs 29:18). Our feelings, as a true source of our visions, are what we create with and our creations are affirmations of our visions. Awakened feelings empower thinking and activity to the point where our thoughts and deeds are our creations. These creative affirmations can take on many spirited forms; even wealth (or, as with George Eastman, its distribution). As physical manifestations, they can exist as cooking, gardening, art, etc.. As deeds they can take the simple form of a lively conversation, a nurturing complement or a beautiful letter. In the case of Antonio Bassolino, a seer with a grand vision, his deeds changed a whole city.

Naples, Italy was a distressed place in 1993 when Bassolino was elected mayor. City government was one big scandal, the economy was in shambles and its public spaces, like its Mediterranean bay, were filled with refuse. Worse yet, its citizens had lost hope. Today all of that has changed. Naples has miraculously become internationally prominent and its citizens have regained hope and new feelings of respected pride in their city thanks to the creative vision of one man.

Bassolino knew Naples for what it once was and for what it could be. Instead of turning to industrial development for growth, as so many cities do, he looked towards the rich cultural heritage of Naples itself. His visions were human and centered around the culture of his people. In being human in purpose they had to be human, not industrial, in practice.

The human core of his vision was simple: the way to make our life a success is to be ourselves. With the human wisdom of his vision Naples became herself. Under his guidance its vast historical wealth was transformed and returned to its citizens. Museums, parks, gardens, streets, squares, courtyards and fountains that were once closed and run-down were cleaned and reopened. Architectural and archaeological wonders were restored to their former splendor. Artistic events, exhibits and festivals abound. This beautiful and vibrant city is now a significant center for greatness in both the arts and tourism. More than just a successful model for development, what it demonstrates is that a vision, wisely embraced, generates the dynamics for responsible change.

In 1948 a small women with a large vision came to the city of Calcutta in India. Her vision was a humanitarian one: to give dignity and care to the abandoned poor, sick and dying. Her name was Sister Teresa. Today we admiringly know her as Mother Teresa: a humble women with great faith, devotion and courage. Initially, she faced harsh abuse and alienation from the neighborhoods in which she worked, but in time came to be viewed as a living saint. In 1979 she was granted the Nobel Peace Prize out of a universal vision that without poverty peace is found at every turn. At the time of her death, at age 87, she had created over 550 Missionaries of Charity world wide, but more than anything else her vision, which she exemplified in her life, became a message for the rest of humanity; a crucial if not fixing marker on the path of excepting our human togetherness.

From just these few examples you can readily see how visions establish a framework; a defining context, in which to do one's work. Visions transport us to the center of ourselves. They relocate the uniqueness of our own perspective and focus creative energies entirely on what is true to our nature. In so doing they attain our purpose by keeping our spirit alive and responsive.

Within the concentrated confines of a vision we have both the freedom and security to creatively bounce ourselves back and forth, up and down; in and out until the dynamics of new possibilities occur. Without the limitations of a vision to live inside of we are less able to meet the intrinsic greatness of our own being and more likely to rely on external influences and give the qualities of others precedence over our own.

7

Integrity

The faces of spirit are many, and when it comes to creative expression integrity is, indeed, a very important countenance. Integrity plays the highest role in bringing wisdom, truth and meaning to human creativity. Works of art: painting, sculpture, pottery, dance, literature, poetry, film, theater, music, etc. find their deepest value as a celebration of integrity. Integrity is what gives direction to human creativity. As our personal truth, it is also our creative truth.

The word itself symbolizes trust and honesty, confidence and conviction, but when associated with creativity it takes on the identity of a discerning force with incorruptible standards of wholeness. As an artist I have come to the realization that my integrity is a result of an involved effort.

Artists navigate in creative realms by using their integrity to locate the passages of truthfulness. When I seek to express myself creatively I am, more often than not, seeking a more truthful insight into my own person.

As an artist, my creativity puts my integrity to the test. And the truth of what I do becomes a report of who I am. If my external work is an honest engagement of my interior work my art won't be without truth.

As an art educator, more than anything else, my teaching has been based upon respect: a respect for myself and a respect for my students as human being. This respect is all encompassing. It permeates every aspect of my studio/classroom life; it is a part of every interaction I have with students. By far, respect is any person's most powerful means for becoming a successful teacher and providing for effective learning. It is also a critical element to me as an artist, but in a different kind of way. For works of art to be deserving of a similar kind of appreciation and to be received with reverence they need to reflect the truth of the artist—they need to be authentic. And while that individual may not always be seen or known by the viewer, the work most, never-the-less, bear forth the self-sustaining courage of his or her respect of self, as a giver, as well as a respect for the viewer as a receiver. In many ways it is the communication of this element of self which secures spiritual memory and provides the world of art with its heroes, icons and history.

As a teacher, I am especially aware of my role in helping others to recognize the fact that their integrity is key to their creative freedom. That they have it within themselves to embrace the frameworks of this very special aspect of the conscious self that ultimately becomes the door to all their journeys, the path to all their destinations, and the light to all happiness. What I have come to learn about this aspect of the autonomous self, is that it cannot be "taught" as much as it can be "caught."

As a parent, I feel an even greater responsibility to teach the standards, ethics and meaningfulness of integrity to my children so that they, too, can identify its principals and take a perspective stance with intrinsic convictions. Of the five children that I have helped to raise, I have only talked to the youngest two girls directly about the virtues of integrity. And, even than, it didn't seem to be particularly necessary, for they too, as pre-teens, genuinely possessed it in great abundance. Where and when did these five people come to include the relevancy of integrity into their identity? Whereupon did they make this spirit-centered transformation. This was important stuff! Difficult to make succeed!

How did they come to catch onto this aspect of spirit that crosses the entire spectrum of character? True, they caught some of the good stuff from mom and dad but they also were fortunate to have grown-up in the midst of a culture, a society and a community where the cooperative environments of many citizens, teachers and peers understood it, lived it and quietly gave it off. While not inclusive, they were each inspirational bearers of a simple yet sacred responsibility of humanness.

Fairness is also a face of integrity. A useful means I had for helping my children determine the appropriate, sentient response to any number of situations was the same means that I often utilized in my parenting of them: the one universal law, the "Golden Rule"—*do not unto others, what you would not have done to you.* This was no parental cop-out. Although I admit it was an extremely simple tool of rightness, it did work for all of us. Maybe not all of the time, but it did connect us with that which was, in the spiritual sense, just.

If we were to take a moment, and look further behind the unfolding dynamics of personal integrity, we would see, of course, that it is related to spiritual evolution. Nothing in one's life is untouched by spirit. As interdependent beings we are propelled by collective influences that are in intricate relationships to a unified whole. Who and what we are is linked to a universal oneness that is life, which is why integrity is fundamental to our personal awakening. Integrity is our honor. Without it we dishonor ourselves and all that is life. Which is why we demean ourselves whenever we harm, abuse, exploit or pollute. And why, for example, we enrich the reality of ourselves whenever we extend love, forgiveness or appreciation.

The relationship between integrity and the spirit is an equitable one. Whenever the spirit is involved, enlightenment is not achieved by rational thought alone; it develops from a trans-rational place and is simultaneously assisted by a myriad of forces that are interlaced with the grace of sincerity, passionate interpretation and the sublime. Integrity is a reflection of self and, when fully realized, a reflection of love—for self as well as for others. One of my main endeavors as a parent was to express continuous and unconditional love to my children. I knew that if love was absent, integrity would be lacking. If a child's heart is not filled with love, it risks the chances of being filled with negative dispositions; including fear and thus racism, sexism, hate and so on.

Integrity is such a universally valued ideal that we seek it in all of our activities, relationships and institutions. So valued, in fact, that whenever something goes wrong in life it can often be traced to an integrity problem. Theoretical views are of little relevance here, but discerning interpretations are critical. How something with intangible dimensions is interpreted through the interior depths of our being determines how the external is manipulated or created.

Integrity is not laying around waiting to be found. It must be sought and, once found, interpreted. And even though our creative activities in the world are a manifestation of our integrity, and ultimately our spirit, they are of little merit until we have learned to scrutinize and interpret the right and wrong, the good the bad and the ugly or, in short, every emergent detail involved.

Any way you approach it, integrity requires work. Without investigative work we cannot come to the depth of a personal intelligence that honestly mirrors our identity and guides our possibilities. Consider happiness for example. We cannot live in its greatest joys if we do not locate our integrity and lift it up, from darkness into the light. As with many things that were once found in the darkness and brought to the light of consciousness, we have to close our two small eyes and look with a large spirit. With our spirit we can find everything that might matter.

8

Truthfulness

Truth and truthfulness are two important yet entirely different concepts. Truth is objective, while truthfulness is not—it is humanly subjective. One is externally visible; the other is illuminated internally. Each functions in a separate context and each is accessed through different means.

When something is said to be true, it is often quiet easy to directly validate it as being so and to immediately come to a mutual agreement. If I said my cat was sleeping on the steps to your house you could go outside to look for the cat yourself and you would know if I were telling the truth. Because truth is what it is, objectively-bound, it can correspondingly be known. If, on the other hand, I said that my family fills my heart with loving emotions, you would not readily be able to tell if that were true or not true. Could I actually be lying to you? Could my behavior be misleading? You really have no direct or representational way of knowing what my true feelings are concerning the love I find with my family, do you?

You could trust me. In doing so, you could believe that I was being truthful about my feelings for my family. Such trust might exist because of our relationship or your history of knowing me as someone who told the truth; especially when the evidence was there to support it. Still, you could not be totally sure if I had really meant what I had said without the objective accuracy of visual proof. After all, I could even have been lying to my self.

A personal truth is an internal truth. A personal truth is truthfulness, and it may or may not relate to external documentation.

Truthfulness may only be substantiated through perception, interpretation and, in most instances, communication. Therapy, for example, is a form of interpretive communication directed to a truthful awareness of self. But for you to know the depth of my feelings—the truthfulness of my being—we would need to establish some form of dialog for you to gain accountable information from. Likewise, if I wanted to validate the truthfulness of my own feelings I would, with all sincerity and honesty, have to examine the intricacies of my internal states of consciousness.

Creative people are forever making these explanatory journeys into self for the sole purpose of knowing their truth so that it is in line with their creative actions. Why?, because the manifestation of creative truth, like real honesty, is an external expression of the internal self. In this context art might be described as the documentation of a journey into self, an objective truth derived from the truthfulness of a deeply subjective experience.

To be a genuinely creative person you not only need to know the truth of your being, but you need to live it as well.

Knowing your own truth is knowing what is real and what is not real. A creative person does not "fake" the truth of the real: the truth of who they are. To do so would be a rejection of self. Not only would this be a tremendous waste of their human energy, it would be fraud and they would become a victim of the unreal.

Your truth is your personal power. It is the currency of your creativity: the financial energy of every creative action you undertake. You have your truth, your creative power, when you disconnect yourself from external influences and give authority to personal wholeness. Internal resources are invested with a sense of spirit and live with a wisdom of personal truthfulness, exterior forces repress these possessions. They continuously petition the creative will to conform to a self-compromising existence. They seek to control beliefs and behavior: from what we eat to where we sleep. If you have any doubts about this, ask yourself, was your last purchase of clothing influenced by a profession, a social occasion, a fad, a loved one, an advertised image or some subtler but equally motivating factor? A great deal of what we are and what we have committed to is not who we really are.

Again, being creative is knowing who you are. Being creative is being intentional . . . it's not living in unawareness, tailored in the accepted norms of convention. It is not avoiding truth but inhabiting truthfulness.

Knowing truth and creatively expressing truth without worrying how others will react is an honoring of one's personal truth and a display of loyalty to self. To value "being" over "being-in-favor" is the truthfulness of a creative spirit. When we manifest our truth, when our behavior is seen as trustworthy, our creative activities become worthy of respect. As with integrity, truthfulness resides in the essence of things more than it does in the appearances.

Love is also a part of truth consciousness. In fact, love is often viewed as the ultimate truth. As you come to know your own truth, and your truthfulness of self, you build-up an immunity to fear. When fear is absent love is usually present. A loving spirit of truthfulness gives us creative strength. By releasing us from our fears, we have less of a need to direct precious energies towards defensive maneuvers or the acquisition of approval and control. Without expectant needs, truth consciousness becomes creative consciousness.

So out of promise for this major prompting of the spirit—this realization of truthworthiness—your truth admits you into a larger concert hall and ushers you to a place where the orchestra is made up of many instruments and musicians, each playing a shared yet pivotal part to the successful performance of the musical score. Likewise, if you are the music and life the musical composition; your truth is the orchestra.

9

Freedom

Freedom. It's the breath of life to creative living. It is nonvisible, yet it is both the source and the substance of many of life's riches and blessings. One of which is that it allows us to take greater control of our lives.

Within a framework of personal freedom we are neither held back nor limited from harnessing our capabilities and shaping our lives. With freedom we are in charge. The choice to be creative; to be happy is ours.

As I am writing this, I'm very much aware that next week, on the 4th of July, my country will celebrate Independence Day, that special-of-special days when America focuses attention on the freedoms that sustain it and when citizens both thank and honor a constitution that nourishes and protects their freedoms. It is also the day that Gail and I celebrate our wedding anniversary. We chose the fourth to get married on because it symbolized, in part, the strength and wisdom of freedom: a substantive strength of our relationship. We saw ourselves as two people that allowed each other the supportive freedom to know and be themselves. Individually we had the freedom to grow stronger together.

In the light of freedom each of us has an opportunity to see the dynamics of our spiritual attributes and to catch inspirational glimpses of wholeness. As we assimilate our freedom and liberate our spirituality we naturally become more creative individuals; freely touching everything and everyone more deeply.

The warm womb of creativity is freedom. Within a spirit of freedom we are at liberty to express the limits of our true being in a fertile world of unlimited opportunities, a world where process as well as product is valued. While everyone may enjoy the finished product, few know how to appreciate the generative freedom of a process that gives birth to a product: that unknown world of creativity where one ventures into seeking to find and to express personal wholeness. Without the freedom that is spirit, we would be submissive slaves to any number of external restraints and self-imposed shackles. Unable to experience our creative freedom we would remain in the womb—unborn.

There is no creativity without inner freedom. Security and the suppressive bondage of traditional forces continuously make their demands upon our life, but as we come to know and trust ourselves we become connected to personal pathways of resourcefulness and more confident at engaging the imagination for creative solutions to our life's needs. In one sense, whenever we are being freely creative we are being born again. Only now, we are awake to life and able to recognize the full genesis of our birth

Creativity, as a movement into the unknown, requires risk taking. If there is spiritual incarceration, it is passively accompanied by fear and uncertainty, and the freedom to act productively is greatly restricted. Such limitations of freedom are ironic, however, in that the process of creation is always connected to an unknown and risk is always connected to a freedom. By letting go of our fear to risk, we access the freedom of our spirit and activate our creativity. No matter how deep or numerous the fears, we have to put them behind us to bring forth new sensitivities and creative activity.

Freedom exists only to the extent that we surpass fear. The spontaneity of our spiritual freedom is often compromised by fear due to any number of ties we may have to existing occurrences or expectations of future outcomes. If and when we become willing to risk new answers we give ourselves the permission and freedom to create. The catalyst for this permission is, of course, our spirit or, more specifically, that awareness of our universally unique self that is dramatically capable of an infinity of successes.

If risk taking is an aspect of freedom, and if freedom is a channel for creativity, we need to overcome anxiety and dissolve fears of the unknown. The surest way to break free of our internal barriers to creativity is to conquer fear by finding the courage to trust in ourselves. Self-trust not only stirs us to rapture, it takes freedom to new levels.

The difference between trust and non-trust is the difference between being creative and being non-creative. Self-trust affects the way we function creatively in life. It has a crucial impact on every aspect of our existence, from how we are as workers, students, lovers and parents to how we function emotionally, mentally, physically and spiritually.

With faith in one's self and one's abilities, the unknown, that vast void of misgiving, becomes less freighting and more appealing as an expanse of possibilities. The faith and trust that is deep within us is what manages our life. It is self-affirmed in our freedom and self-expressed in our creativity.

When we trust in ourselves we are no longer a prisoner to our fears. Whenever we do an internal change-over, and replace fear with trust, we strengthen the identity of our spirit and give it greater freedom. America's poet laureate Robert Pinsky believes that we free our creativity only by giving up our fears. A creative writing professor at Boston University, Pinsky uses many techniques to help students free themselves from those safe corners of life that fear has backed them into. One of his favorite means for developing "expansive" thinking involves studying the creative achievements of others. By choosing their own creative mentors, students make a stronger connection to the rich energy of their own creative passions. I feel compelled here to use a little poetic imagery and add that by looking into others they polish their own mirror.

Just as America is a country that stands for freedom, trust (as it dissolves insecurities) is a condition of freedom. Freedom is a spirit filled with trust. It is our victor in the battle with our fear. With it we are able to live a life with far fewer conditions, restrictions and illusions. With a trusting spirit we are, quite literally, free to be our natural selves and free to commit our creative energies, with increased imagination, to wherever we choose to apply them. Without a heavy burden of fear, doubt and ignorance we are free, with greater energy, to be in the world but not necessarily of it.

Freedom is also a letting go of our past. To be free in

the present is to be free of the past. Creative beings do not let their past life prevent them from inhabiting the possibilities of their present life. To them life is an invitation. An invitation to consciously choose a creative response to every experience.

Creative people don't trust the status quo as much as they trust in the natural nature of the universe. Being creative is being open to change. When one is open— free of bias and ambivalence—the universe becomes a golden expanse of unending opportunities. Artists spontaneously surrender to these opportunities and recognize them as occurrences which they have the freedom to snatch. They are forever ready to receive a humble thought, an image or an event as an inspiration and to instantly act upon it. Guided by the wisdom of their freedom they have the strength of spirit to know that all will work out well. I use the word "wisdom" because freedom is a great supplier of creativity and that creativity can be a spiritual, mental and physical source for all solutions.

A feeling of excitement flows through one's entire being when they are being creative. Creativity in process is freedom bearing fruit. It is the joy and celebration of a realized self that allows the flame of our spirituality to burn brightly. And, of course, wherever the light of spirit shines it enhances creativity and both bring new meaning into life.

10

Play

"Child's play!" You have, no doubt, heard these words to suggest that some task in life was easy or simple to do, but are you old enough to play again like a child?

Not everyone has had a playful childhood. Many don't experience the awe of enchanted lands, colorful wizards, summer sounds, sun-filled rooms, love affairs with *Snow White, Robin Hood, Bambi* or any number of other valiant characters as children. For many, the fire, the madness, the magic, the innocence, the dreams and the unending intoxication with activities that are indescribable but for the words "child's play", are not experienced until much later in life.

In our minds, we're never far from the desire to reconnect with positive childhood feelings, whether they be ones we actually experienced or those we can only have wished for. Silently, almost in secret, we carry their sweetness with us wherever we go. Hoping someday to spontaneously relive them or, in some magical way, live them for the first time.

Pablo Picasso said that it took a long time to become a child. What he meant was that it can take a long time to find the craving curiosity, invincible courage and playful freedom we identified ourselves with as children but may have forgotten or lost as adults. The playful spirit that was ours as children, remembered or not, has played a continuous role in shaping our lives. The spirit of play is with us still. It may not be as fresh and gentle as we once knew it, but it remains a natural pathway to the imagination. The mature side of Picasso the artist, is the creative side of Picasso the child. His work has little to do with chronological age and much to do with child-like genius. It is true, you see, children are naturally creative artists.

Play is an instinctive and elemental phenomenon of the human spirit.

In any form, play is intuitive creativity in action. Inherent in our being is a vast plurality of feelings, images and intuitive responses that originate from the deepest levels of our inner knowledge. Through the freedom of play we are able to penetrate these levels and tap into the guiding force of our own knowledge . . . our own creative self.

As an activity, play is a flexible way of doing something, but it is also a frame of mind and as such becomes an evolutionary source for all that is original. Play is also spiritual in a highly personal context that is both sacred and divine in its relationship to ourselves and our work. In one sense it is the spiritual wisdom of our subconscious—of our very being.

Play is creative work. With a spectacular spectrum of freedoms, it draws on our personal passions and intuitive feelings, leading us to new insights. Such breakthroughs are to be treasured in that they ultimately provide the new sources, the life giving origins, for our everyday work.

Play is the spirit shepherd of metamorphosis. Through play, activity becomes a process of passion. Through play we become intrinsically motivated to be creative out of the pure, simple joy of doing rather than for any extrinsic compensation.

The disciplines of Zen Buddhism, which center around the attainment of enlightenment through self-knowledge, have long suggested that we look within ourselves for the knowledge and peace needed to live in spiritual equilibrium. Through the universal language of play our capacities, as people seeking to be more creative, are seeded with personal insights and fertilized with an excitement of freedom. Through play we are able to take hold of our reality and find our creative voice. The Zen concept of the universal self suggests that by letting go, by doing without thinking, we merge with the doing and find our freedom. Through such transformations a person's entire life becomes a creative mosaic and every expression a creative act. Because playing is a form of unhindered doing it is relatively free of attachment and rises beyond any psychological need for control.

An exciting aspect of playing in this manner is that no initial expectations concerning a grandiose or artistic end results exist. The inhibiting pressures of common adult psychological forces, such as preconceptions, critical judgments and ego controls, don't have the time to surface when the activity is seemingly informal or playfully structured. Extremely valuable things develop that can sweep across whole new horizons when life is playfully engaged.

Due to individual personality traits its not easy to assess just how far we are able to realize our creative powers through play. For some, resistance may arise out of personal fears or a need for intellectual grounding. For others, more trusting in nature and less anxious about taking risks, play experiences may prove to be more rewarding. Initially, such experiences are less anxious when familiar activities are dealt with. Once the known is approached in a playful manner many fears and obstacles are transformed and, minute-by-minute, the play activity itself releases natural desires to be creative in ways that, although maybe not new to the world, are freeing to the participant.

Playing, like any process or technique, is something we use when being creative but it is not what we create with: it is not our creative force. If we were to let either play or some other external circumstance direct our work we would be surrendering our personal vision and any hope for self-realization along with it. What our creativeness can bring forth already exists within us. It will be an extension of who we are. For example, you may not yet know what will give birth to your next endeavor, but in one form or another it is you who will be its living source and it will be you who will body it forth. Likewise, you may not know today what you will be choosing for dinner tomorrow but you will choose something. With playing, we can dismantle the obstacles of psychic obstruction. When it comes to freeing up the creative spirit, play provides some of the therapeutic tools, the screw divers, the pliers and the wrenches, for loosening the fasteners of repressedness. Once some of these personal blocks are removed the creative process becomes a powerful resource for experiencing personal wholeness.

When we play we make new discoveries and often find ourselves in places where we are given new views to our true identity. Out of the surprises and excitement of play travel we re-create new ways in which to structure our lives.

11

Trust

Creativity in life is a personal expression of trust. Being creative means trusting in the experience of your own process: in the living of your life. Artists, for example, have to live in trust. Trusting is a conscious part of their being. It is the content of their own unfolding; their leading voice of truth. For artists trust is a necessity. It's what carries their life and their work forth. Without it they are far removed from sensations of spirit and realities of visions. While with it, their inner life is empowered and willing to pay homage to the unknown. With trust they have the clarity of spirit to act.

Creative people often experience the uncertainty of

living in and with the unknown. This is, however, not necessarily a frightening state of being. For anyone with the courage to embrace their own individual truth the unknown can simply be a welcoming scene where they continuously receive life's most fulfilling rewards. To always live in the known, on the other hand, is a reproduction of what once existed but repetition is not creation. Creativity always yields a new and uniquely different result with each and every act. If it's not different it's not creative. If it has previously occurred it resides in the realm of the known and neither its legacy or one's existence is meaningfully expanded by its recreation. Ultimately, the known becomes spiritually more freighting and much less tempting that the unknown.

Spirituality is the unknown mystery of our center. It does not exist for itself but for our fulfillment. Our spirit is larger than our personal turmoils. As a conditionless presence it gracefully keeps us in trust and holds us close to the heart. Creativity is the known reality of our center. It is the coalescent source of our emergence. As the origin of our visions, it allows us to do our best. One continuously nurtures who we are the other cultivates what we do, giving imaginative birth to expression. Both forces direct us toward trust and, for that reason if for no other, are to be honored equally.

Creativity is that mysterious ability to provide whatever is required of a present circumstance. It is a natural process, served not as much by deliberation as by trust. In other words it is passively active rather than an ambitiously controlled pursuit. A move of spontaneity, of confidence, of strength. A continuous move of trust receiving trust.

Of itself, creativity has no attachment, desire, mind set or agenda. It is without motive, yet endless in its usefulness. Birthing and nourishing are its primal and honored virtues. Its gentle essence is the root of all accomplishments great and small, joyful and sorrowful; lasting and temporal. All of these generous things, be they bad or good, are made possible through the expansive guidance of trust.

With trust living is easy. The more one experiences their creative gifts and integrates them into their day-to-day routines, the less intimidating life appears. Creativeness springs from trust, but trust is also a reward that being creative bestows upon us. Once trust, the greatest gift that being creative has to offer, becomes our partner, our ally, life and all of its surprises are met with confidence. Fears or anxieties about change, loss and adversity no longer emerge as forces capable of working against our happiness. What does surface is the delivering energy of trust. Its strength fuses with the fullness of our potential, and together creativity and trust are capable of resolving most cares. This brave faith in one's creative potential to reverse difficulties serves us more than thinking itself.

Trust occupies a place deep within our unconsciousness yet is the companion to each creative act we perform in the world. We are the shadow to its every move. To realize our capacity for self trust we need to look inside ourselves. Trust is an internal knowing, a gift of the spirit that is slowly yet constantly revealed to us. It is a friendly gift. And the more we recognize its loving personality the more we will come to know it as a shepherd to our humanness; the origin of our creativity. This private presence is the most valuable possession that an individual could possibly receive. It is the unseen crown of wisdom itself. Hidden from others to see, it is an elaborate power for you to honor and to carry forth into life. With it you are in charge. You have freedom: creative freedom!

In any number of ways, trust is how we come to know ourselves. In the same way that it helps us to know our freedom, it can also lead us to the treasure of our own truth.

Aristotle's writings, especially the *Nicomachean Ethics*, have intellectually influenced the progress of humanity for centuries. This classical Greek philosopher, once a student of Plato, concluded that a life devoted to seeking truth and expressing truth was the highest of virtuous activities. As one of the world' greatest thinkers he cautioned us not to follow the advise of others or to think in mortal terms, " . . . but must, so far as we can, make ourselves immortal, and strain every nerve to live in accordance with the best thing in us; for even if it be small in bulk, much more does it in power and worth surpass everything."

There are plenty of ways to take in and reflect upon the meaning of Aristotle's shared words. Philosophy, in general, is both very far-reaching and very curbing. Whether we like it or not, however, it does generate a poetic measure of consciousness. We ponder. We penetrate. A new truth may take shape inside us. An inner truth of self that we can trust. An envisioning trust that we can live within and creatively respond to. Even today we grow and aspire as Aristotle redelivers a simple yet discriminating message: to trust in our own truth.

With trust, an individual's creativity can never be held captive. Its qualities are luminous and shine where there is communal darkness. As a quality of leadership, trust is the creative light that shows the way to new ways of living. It is the illuminating path into the unknown. Painter Richard Diebenkorn's, in his notes to himself on beginning a painting, wrote: "Attempt what is not certain", to remind himself that certainty might be a delusion and that he needs to remain comfortable with consummating his own truths.

Trust does not condescend. It is not prideful but

rather a humble teacher. A very polite and courteous instructor of personal truths. Trust is also a spiritual servant, a giving caretaker, with no selfish longings, who opens doors when we knock and lends a hand when ours are much too full of unmarked packages.

Our trust is also our balance. Without it we falter. It keeps us upright and moving without swaying. The way we become creatively upright and centered in our life is the way we greet trust and accept its support. Where living is fortified with a spreading spirit of trust, creativity flourishes.

12

Self-Esteem

Self-esteem is feeling worthy of one's personal gifts while at the same time regarding them as an extraordinary treasure. Esteem of self is a respect of self. It is what awakens our spirit and directs our creativity, allowing each of us to live a wide life instead of a narrow one.

I often tell my students that self-esteem is the primal source of creativity and in my book *The Spirit of Clay* devoted a section to it under the heading "The Mysteries of Creativity", part of which I'd like to share with you here:

The mysteries of the creative self are intimate and closely allied to the mysteries of love, health and happiness in that they center around positive self-esteem as a fundamental element of human evolution. To have a truly successful and happy relationship with clay, as with a friend or loved one, we must not only be consciously aware of who we are and what we are doing but also confident with that awareness of self. It is the one indispensable key to creatively meeting the challenges that continuously present themselves to us.

Our belief in ourselves is the immune system of the spirit. It energizes and empowers our thoughts and actions by providing the psychological strength and healthy resilience to prevent life from becoming a frightening experience.

When self-esteem is low a confining fear dominates all that we do. Insecurity and uncertainty become expansive and the safety of the known and the familiar is embraced. In such a noninspiring state change is avoided and inactivity courted. Creatively, this is a toxic and invalidating existence where personal values, aspirations and feelings cannot be honored yet alone expressed.

High self-esteem, on the other hand, is a highly motivating force. When our self-esteem is strong and positive we seek to experience life (on all levels) in a more active and fulfilling manner. Creatively we seek to express the joy and bountifulness that lives within us. In this sense creativity is a celebrative signature, an affirmation, of our self-assurance.

When we believe in ourselves to the very center of our being, we become more compassionate and respectful of just who it is that we are. With this magnitude of self-acceptance not only are we able to be more assertive in expressing ourselves, but we are able to do so in cherished ways that are highly creative. Positive feelings of self-respect, in addition to allowing us to live more creatively, allow us also to live more purposefully and with greater personal integrity.

Creative activity is a reflection of self-hood; it is a window into an individual's sense of being. When we are being creative we are living within a wholeness of self. Being creative is an activity of integration where our physical, mental and spiritual strengths come together in praise and thanksgiving.

Creativity is also a standard for measuring our overall well-being. I once remarked to one of my most respected teaching colleagues, John Pappas, that a number of my students that semester seemed more committed to healing themselves through ceramics than to being artistic. His immediate, and off-handed reply was that the entire art department was a therapy center. In so many ways his comment was right on the mark. Art departments and art schools are awesome places of personal empowerment.

Whenever we have the opportunity to be creative we

have the opportunity to discover and develop a greater sense of self—a sense of self that is spiritually expanded. It seems that the medical professions are just now beginning to realize that emotional and physical illness can be directly related to the health of one's spirit. I think, for the most part, that artists have always been aware of this connection. Maybe not always consciously, but their context for being expressive was never one of spiritual numbness.

Being creative does not necessarily guarantee a happy existence. Many creative people are like the fabled Zen master who attained enlightenment, only to discover that he was still as miserable as before. Artists, like enlightened Buddhists, have no special claims on happiness or freedom from pain. It's just that they might have been worse off had they not been able, on behalf of their creative awareness, to find their spiritual paths.

Positive self esteem is, and always has been, a marvelously healing force. Its liberating powers expand creative consciousness and can lead us closer to the path of our own spirituality. How we think and feel about ourselves is not only important to how we find this path but also to how we transform self into creative achievement. We have a choice to be positive and upbeat just as we have a choice to be negative and cynical. If we don't feel the fellowship of healthy and successful visions of self how can we feel creative?

Confidence in one's self generates creative thinking. If we don't already embrace a respected vision of self, there are a few basic ways in which to advance one.

One major way is to avoid negativity. It is very easy to surrender to adversity and to let haunting fears get to us. Negative circumstances, like negative surroundings and support, are highly toxic and easily harm us. They breed self doubt and wound us with barbs of inferiority. Our defense is not to submit to them but to remain positive. We don't necessarily need to transform such constrictions as much as we need to dissolve them by seeing the hidden dynamics of positive possibilities and celebrating those qualities.

Defeat, like negativity, lowers self-esteem. But a set back is only a failure if it is accepted as a failure. Mistakes are a part of life and an even bigger part of creative processes, just don't let them discourage you. Use mistakes as valuable teaching lessons. Instead of acknowledging defeat acknowledge that pulsing inner courage that resides deep inside. Feel its silent strength. Its there, only you have to find the courage to overcome the obstacles and to persevere.

Another important way is to avoid passivity. Don't sit around waiting for miracles to happen. Why? Because they are not going to come if you don't personally generate them or feel deserving of them. While it is easier to take a "passive" rather than an "active" approach to living, the miracles in life only happen when we assert ourselves.

If, in general, we don't feel confident with certain aspects of ourselves, we are more likely to avoid being active in those same areas of our life. As a result, we become the victims of our own inactivity. If, on the other hand, we choose (and it is always a choice) to become actively responsible for our lives we will, in essence, literally create our own miracles. Just as living actively is linked to self-responsibility, living creatively is linked to self-esteem.

A pro-active approach to living gives more meaning to our existence; it prepares the way for the uniqueness of our humanness and the rewards of our own creativity. As our level of consciousness rises so does our confidence. Self-confidence is an empowering gift. Used responsibly it can be used to honor ourselves, used creatively it can be offered as a gift to the life experience of others.

13

Identity

Our identity is a collection of characteristics that we come to know ourselves through. It is also a way that we are known to others. The more we are able to discover our identity, the more we are able to live within it and creatively direct our lives.

In our understanding of self, we learn a basic respect not only for ourselves but for all those influences that surround our lives. As our identity evolves we can recognize many of life's interconnecting relationships, and our spirits deepen. In time, we may come to realize our oneness with all the forces of the universe—and a stable peace of spiritual tranquillity.

Our personality is not our identity. Our identity reveals the body of our spirit in all of its muscular detail, whereas personality is the clothing covering that body. If identity is the depth of spirit, personality is a glimpse of it: a surface appraisal.

We honor ourselves when we honor the contributions of the spirit and creatively connect them to every aspect of our life. The textural composition of individual identity, in turn, inspires the fabric of our living to where we bring spirit into everything we do. In essence then, we use spirit (the spirit of our identity) to create spirit. Who we are and what we do form a unitary blend . . . become one. Spirit begets spirit and separation ceases.

Our individual identity is part of our collective identity. Art, for example, is conceived from an aesthetic identity that represents various expressions of personal truths and exists as a collective identity when it contextually connects with those same understanding in others. These shared connections may be both conscious and unconscious but they are always subjective. The closer connections come to addressing meaningful truths of common understanding the more value they attract.

When we speak of identity in relation to a collective identity we can easily get hooked up with any number of organized norms and institutions that define a society or a culture—including morals and ethics. Collective identities embrace morality. You might even think of moral sensibilities as a social adhesive. Identity may result as a manifestation of spirit but morals do not. Morality is a form of collective consciousness and as such seeks truth and judgment through ethical principles that are universal.

Our identity acknowledges morality when it acknowledges a responsibility for others. Like creativity, it is a discreet and sensitive form of identity consciousness that knows what's right. Connected to the spirit of our identity we are more knowingly able to recognize the limits of rational definitions and the need for human responses. While the concepts of love are important to creation they are central to a morality of truthfulness. Without love there is no moral imperative.

Correspondingly, if our identity is intricately linked with love and moral understanding we are in a position to live with integrity and experience our spirit with a real rather than false sense of passion. We need to know our real passion. Not knowing the truthfulness of passions we could easily waste away our special talents without ever having made creative use of them. When this happens, great harm is done to the individual who is not able to creatively live their life doing what they passionately believe in. Children, for example, are often at risk of being grievously guided (pushed might be an accurate word in some instances) into living a life that does not acknowledge their personal uniqueness or fit their individual interests. For example, a tragic consequence of forced parental vision is emotionally brought to our live's in the well-known movie *"Dead Poet's Society"* when one member of the cast's starring group of students is made to leave school at the precise moment his consciousness of others is expanded and he experiences his real identity and creative skills. The temperament, needs and interests of the overbearing father so overpower those of the son's that he sees no hope for his own identity and, in the depths of frustration, ends his life with his father's own hand gun.

One seemingly consistent characteristic of identity in creative people is that as children they had an independence to both discover and pursue their interests with a true spirit of passion. What is most necessary for creative people, children and adults alike, is that they develop a reliable sense of self as a responsive base from which to act. Identity is a universal context for creative living. If we acknowledge a true sense of self, irregardless of our individual life circumstances, we are able to maintain at all times a creative relationship with life. If, on the other hand, we suspend trust and relinquish knowledge of self then every challenge life presents to us becomes a missed creative opportunity and experience of enjoyment.

Every experience in life can be a favorable occasion

through which to manifest our creativity and to delight in our uniqueness if we accept the personal dynamics of our genuine selves. To be genuinely creative we need to be most responsive to our authentic identity in every situation and least responsive to the identities that our roles in life provide us with. As an American male, for example, I recognize my role as a husband and identify with many of its loving elements but what really accounts for the depth of intimacy, commitment and love that I have for Gail, my wife, is rooted in the high-esteem and active understanding of my own individual identity. Our love relationship is made that much more fulfilling, of course, due to Gail's acceptance of her own unique identity. Individuals who accept their own identities as well as those of their partners bring out the best in each other and in the relationship. Self identity is an ingredient that somehow makes it feel wonderful and right.

Likewise, as an artist my work is strongest when it evolves from energies enhanced by the creative freedoms granted by a knowledge of self. If the capacity of that personal freedom were to be limited by a less than healthy sense of self I would most certainly feel less than content. To be a good husband, artist, or whatever, one must respect and trust in themselves. A beloved identity affirms individuality and allows for creative exploration.

14

Courage

It is important to know who you are to know what is right but it is also important to act on what you know. As a spirit-filled willingness to act upon what is known to be right, courage is a blending of character and action. In the same way that courtesy is the heart of civility, courage is the force that unites creativity with productive living.

Courage in life and creative activity are inseparable. In the same way that creative action inspires further creativity, courageous activity generates additional courage. The amount of creative energy that any individual has in their life is ultimately dependent on the amount of courage they posses.

Creativity is a triumph of courage. The creative talents people have are the ones they had the courage to realize. Courageous people are pro-active, which is to say that they act and are not just acted upon. They are also people who are centered around their spirit and focused upon their values. One's spirit and values are the magical ingredients that go into the formulation of personal courage. They provide the truth and standards of leadership needed to define the appropriate answer, the right course of action and the motivation to prevail.

Whenever I think of courage I remember a moving story that I have come to honor as a symbol of courage. A story that reminds me that everyone carries around translucent wings, representing the ability to make clear choices irregardless of circumstances, that somehow lift us upward at the right moment and allow us to soar, reunited, with our spirit.

While serving as a United States Senator in the early 1950's John F. Kennedy, who would be elected President of the United States in 1960, wrote the Pulitzer Prize—winning *Profiles in Courage*. In this book, which was written while recovering from major back surgery, Kennedy illuminates eight political personalities, each a U. S. Senator, who heroically displayed a more than an admirable amount of courage—which he, himself, once defined as "Grace under pressure." One of his profiles focused on Edmund G. Ross, a man who's courage not only saved a U. S. President from impeachment but may also have saved the Presidency as an institution as well. Every day stories of personal courage arise . . . but this heroic story is well over a hundred years old.

In 1868 the Republican leaders of Congress sought to govern the defeated South as conquered states, while then President Andrew Johnson sought reconciliation. He vetoed so many Legislative bills on the basis of their unconstitutionality and severity toward the South that Congress set out with a vengeance to impeach Johnson and remove him from office. The House passed the impeachment resolution but when it came to the Senate the Republicans, realizing, to everyone's dismay, that they were one vote short of a two thirds majority, put every means of personal and political pressure available to them on Edmund G. Ross, their colleague form Kansas, to obtain his crucial vote.

Senator Ross was, himself, a Republican. He was openly opposed to Andrew Johnson and his political policies but when he recognized that Johnson was going to receive a political trial instead of a fair trial, he refused to commit his vote during a preliminary poll.

Ross made the courageous choice to stand alone as an individual rather than as a majority with his party. In a moment of national crisis he had the courage to put a public interest ahead of a private or political one.

Ross was harangued daily and besieged by criticism, appeals, threats and bribes. He was mercilessly dishonored by his party and country. On the morning of his fateful vote, he felt that he was literally looking into his own grave with everything that made life inviting about to be lost forever in the utterance of two words: "not guilty". After the vote Ross's political life ended. Fellow Congressmen denounced him and millions of citizens viewed him with contempt. He served out his term as "Traitor Ross", was not re-elected and returned to Kansas where he endured ostracism and poverty.

Many years later, just before his death, Ross received tribute in the press for his act of consciousness in saving the government from mob rule and the country from a fate worse than war. His courage saved the office of the U. S. Presidency from partisan control and democracy from autocracy. But how do the complexities of courage in politics differ from those in everyday life? Well, they don't, it's just that results aren't always as recognizable.

Courage can be explained through many examples, by men such as Senator Ross, but its source is less explainable. How one comes to find courage in life is unique to every individual. John F. Kennedy said that we find it by looking into our own soul. If we do look inside, if we see our spirit and if we like what we see, then at various times in our life the gift of our courage and the possibilities of its power are revealed to us.

Our courage will show itself to us to the degree that we value and respect our own spirit. Our love for ourselves, and all that we hold dear, is what gives us the courage to act with out fear of consequence. It is what allows us the freedom to sing, dance, act, paint, or whatever, as if nobody is watching.

Courage outweighs inhibition of any kind. With limited self love comes limited courage. Without a healthy love of self, one looks externally for approval and satisfaction: places where courage and conscience do not travel. Self-esteem and courage are omnipotent and are found on the same path. When they unite a, stronger, more creative spirit emerges.

15

Attitude

If you think you can—you can, said Henry Ford, and if you think you can't—you can't. What this famous observation by Ford describes is a simple, yet significant, prerequisite to creative action. A spirit tempered by an optimistic and positive attitude is a spirit that sparkles with ideas and imagination. It is a bright spirit that radiates with spontaneity. It is, altogether, a spirit primed for creative achievement.

Our attitude, like our behavior, is a reflection of our self-image. And, whether we like it or not, it controls our destiny through the two universal laws of attraction. Laws which mainly confirm that negative thinking, habits, etc. generate negative results and that positive thoughts originate positive results.

Our attitude is also our perception of life. We don't find our creative successes and happiness through what life brings us as much as we do through how we perceive life's happenings. John Milton wrote, "The mind is its own place, and can make a heaven of hell or a hell of heaven." With the help of the spirit, we are able to see life through the wonder of who we are and to make it a haven of positive possibilities capable of generating forces of creative motion. Thomas Edison, a close friend of Henry Ford and the owner of eleven hundred patents, tested thousands of materials and material combinations before discovering an electrical resistance filament for his light bulb. When asked why he continued after so many failures, he answered, I haven't failed once—for 9,000 times I learned what didn't work.

To be a creative individual and to find purpose in life one may not necessarily need to change what one is doing, only alter the way one thinks about it. When it comes to creativity and a spirit-filled life, our feelings become every bit as important as our activities. Creatively, there is a duality that emanates between thought and action. During times of difficulty and reexamination (those periods of personal struggle laced with ignorance as well as a disillusionment of knowledge) the nature of that duality becomes severely distorted as does reality in general. What supports you here, and helps your spirit to survive, is your attitude. It can become the wisdom map for the spirit and the leading guide to your creative uniqueness and, hopefully, your true calling.

There are many factors that affect our creative behavior and creative living. Our environments, our personality, our individual assets in the form of interests, skills, talents and so on reveal what we can do, but it is our attitude that determines what we will do.

With the right attitude, joy and excitement can accompany your every activity. Ultimately, it can lead you to yourself. With a loving attitude, for example, self-forgiveness, trust, courage and any number of spiritual ingredients pass through you that not only enable you to be a more compassionate person but a profoundly creative one as well. In a fundamental sense, creative consciousness is so intricately linked to one's self awareness that it is both identified and validated by one's attitude. As we recognize the uniqueness of our individual abilities and embrace those talents that distinguish us from others, it should come as no surprise when our acts of expression result in unique expressions of self that are fully creative and, most importantly, deeply satisfying.

My father told me that life was 50% attitude. He must have wanted my initiation in this matter to be secure, as he repeated it often. I wish now that he had spent more time explaining what made up the other half of life, but then again maybe that is part of a father's intention: for his children to tangle with life, dissolve its mysteries and to, eventually, accept their own spirit.

Charles Swindoll is an even stronger advocate of attitude. He believes that " . . . life is 10 percent what happens to us and 90 percent how we respond to it." He places attitude above education, wealth and success. It is so important, that he is convinced it can make or break just about any earnest endeavor in life.

I am very conscientious of my attitude as a citizen, teacher, artist, parent, husband and so on, because I steadfastly acknowledge my attitude as a primary embracer of life. It is a mutual embrace—life and my attitude towards it are always submitting to each other; are forever accepting of a natural bond. Together they mark the difference between significance and insignificance. What I do as a creative person can rise in purity and throb with essence or exist as nothingness: remaining lost and bewildered. What I do is a sacred reflection of my attitude, and that reflection becomes my art, my love and my life. The way I make a piece of pottery is the way life will embrace me.

I have a long-time favorite saying which my students and children know all-to-well. You too may groan . . . but here it is: *"life can be delish with a sunny disposish."* It's one of those "outlook" equals "outcome" kind of sayings meant to restore balance and bring clarity to living, yet I always found it insightful in a light-hearted way. It always drew smiles but somehow I sensed it always delivered its message when needed, and when was it needed? Whenever someone couldn't change their reality and had to change their perspective.

Changes of attitude come from living. They don't come from institutions, doctrines, philosophies and books. Day by day, minute by minute they are made known to us. Spiritually and creatively these are the real changes that become our rites of passage to wholeness. There are two components to this form of change: the first is awareness and the second is acceptance. For a change in attitude to occur we have to recognize a personal need for redirecting values and then we must allow those values to be put into practice. When a desire to effect change results from a loving or compassionate need the results can be much deeper and longer lasting than if they originated for self-serving reasons. Whenever attitude is connected to the spirit a great number of potential conflicts in our life are eliminated. A lot of goodness and peacefulness is associated with the nature of the spirit and, when that spirit is a part of the change we experience, a natural sense of wholeness unfolds within us. Lacking ego and arrogance, the spirit is a great ally of a healthy attitude.

16

Faith

In the realm of the spirit, faith is a trusting response of our capabilities to creatively resolve our needs. It is the security and manifestation of our courage to believe in our own actions . . . whatever the outcome. Through the spirit of faith we own trust. A trust that is simultaneously vulnerable and unassailable. In faith there is always the risk of the nonsuccesses but, irregardless of any mishaps, there remains an unfailing assuredness of self.

In spirit faith the self is the source for trusting in one's self. Unlike religious faith, there is no spiritual go-between, no constructed spiritual scaffolding, for one's faith to be entrusted too. Faith, as a gift of the spirit, is a healthy emotional bounding with self. It is an affirmation of personal power and belief. It affirms an identity of the self with the knowledge that "I am my own person." In so doing it acknowledges that one knows what is and what isn't important. Likewise, it recognizes what one needs, wants and is capable of. Such an individualized faith need not be detached from religion. Often it appreciates, pursues, embodies and coexists with its interests. Yet the path to a personal faith rooted in self-freedom is a pilgrimage of a different kind. The journey towards a faith characterized by personal spirit takes a great deal of effort. Its beginnings require self-knowledge, self-love, intuition and caring. As one's faith grows in character, the strength and willingness to move to new ground is an unfolding sign of spiritual understanding and connectedness.

Jackson Pollock displayed a tremendous amount of personal faith when, in the 1950's, he sought a painterly form of expression that was consistent with the times in which he lived and not dependent on those of the past. He set a new precedent in large scale painting by literally bringing the canvas off the easel and onto the floor where it could be painted with a stick (as opposed to a brush) using the movements of his whole body and not just those of his wrist. As an "Action Painter", he didn't feel the need to go outside of himself for the images of his subject matter. He worked, trustingly, from within.

He didn't use still-lifes, nude models or even sketches—
he worked directly within the vibrant dynamics of the
moment and in harmony with his convictions. His art is
buoyant with confidence and alive with faithfulness . . .
very exciting stuff!

Faith is also a spiritual commitment to our real self. It
honors our true nature by liberating us from the manip-
ulation of the ego and personal ambivalence. Faith respects our true self by supporting the uniqueness of our
individual perspectives. Pollock was able to create the
way he did because his faith allowed for a different perspective. Where others were placing "question marks" or
making mountains out of mole hills of doubt, he put his
faith into action and added one heroically aesthetic "pe-
riod" to the world of modern art. Pollock, like anyone
who becomes an achiever because they were a believer,
moved a mountain.

Without a spiritual faith in our own creativity we are
lost to a faith of noncreativity. As an inner awareness,
faith is a sense of things beyond our rational knowing.
Connected to our spirit, it is a miraculous part of our
being; of everyone's being. Because something may not
be readily accessible to us does not mean that it's nonex-
istent. Creativity is a natural gift within us. Whether we
choose to believe in it, and acknowledge it, is a choice of
faith that is up to each of us. And, as a human phenomena, that's what being creative is: having faith in one's

own self. As a visionary treasure of the spirit, faith is our orientation to a creative future.

To claim our natural connection to our creative destiny we must maintain an ongoing openness with the faith we have within ourselves. Our faith is our refuge. It keeps our insecurities at bay, leaving us free to act without tripping over barriers of self-denial and barricades of self-doubt. For creative action to occur we don't need to acquire a whole range of new skills, we only need to abandon a wide range of old images.

"Often I think of us as the earth itself," Anaïs Nin once wrote, "full of hidden treasures . . . all subterranean and having to be brought to the surface". Like creativity, the precious riches of our spirit can only surface when we are awake to the truth of our own being. We cannot keep the self locked away in dark places of untruth while, at the same time, expecting to do extraordinary things.

Faith is a translator for the spirit. When we do something that is essentially unique, it is often a consequence of our faith transforming spirit energy into creative energy through an expanded vocabulary of self. Without the motivating power of faith the self is seldom strong enough to cultivate responses to living that are authentic. In many ways, our faith is a spiritual channel for our imagination. It is deeply symbolic of the respect we have for ourselves and out of that respect it provides more skillful assistance to our visionary accomplishments than we generally give it credit for.

Without wanting to sound idealistic, there is a growing consequence to faith that occurs naturally. When we find faith in ourselves we can find it in others. The human dimensions of this cycle is not without its rewards. In addition to providing new openings for intimacy and community, we form a new basis for equality. It was once said by William Hazlitt that those who are at war with others are not at peace with themselves. With the transformative blessings of our faith, we are better able to find a personal peace that can be a source for spiritual bonding and a much larger peace in the world. Unpretending faith will reveal itself in everything we do if it is a part of everything we are. As an invisible gateway between shadows and sunshine, between the impossible and the possible, faith is indispensable.

17

Passion

We've all experienced overwhelming emotions for someone or for something. At times our responsiveness may have contained such enthusiasm that our normal state of being was unable to handle the excitement. Such intense feelings and strong expressions of self are not unusual to the human condition. In fact, they renew life and constitute the origins for a more creative reality. This inner genius of our spirit has been called an "essential condition" but most of us simply know this zesty form of wisdom as passion.

Passion is a creative life resource. It enhances the flow of spiritual energy bringing vitality to our being. It becomes both teacher and guide. Once we understand its potential to move through us and become a component of our expression we can trust in its ability to reveal elevated dimensions of creativity. When we accept passion as a primal force for internal change, we access a natural freedom that is ours alone and that allows being creative to be forever within our reach.

Creativity is an odd yet natural embrace with the intelligence of awareness. The more deeply aware we are of the nature of passion and its relationship to the spirit and to living, the more resourceful we become with our creative gifts.

Passion, as an energy of personal awareness, is the love and spirit that we bring to our life. Artistically, it is an invisible energy that gives visible form to our expression and expression to all of our forms. Passion is—next to love—perhaps the second most insistent and powerful force in life. Through passion human creativity not only finds direction, but depth as well. Henri Matisse, without a doubt my favorite painter, single-handedly changed the world of contemporary art through his passion for color. He once said, from the outset, that everything he felt and did was through color. Through out his life he remained faithful to this singular passion, tirelessly dedicating himself to the sensuous articulation of color's artistic force. The elusive miracle of Matisse to saturate color with energy and spirit, unmistakably, re-defined the nature of color itself.

Passion is also power, a very forceful energizer. It makes dreams, outfits journeys, puts paint on canvas and so on. Passion is what separates similar forms of expressions: one painting from another painting. Two people, for example, can paint the same still-life, portrait or landscape, yet the results will differ. One painter may react to the subject being painted with a sense of personal exuberance; the other as a technical challenge. In the painting, both become transparent and reveal their degree of intimacy with self and with life. Just as an individual artist has the ability to turn paint into expression, personal passion has the ability to turn living into an imaginatively creative and inspiring experience.

Creative energy is the vibrant energy of passion. It is a major source of our personal power and connects us with the supportive powers of our spirit and of the universe around us. Without passion everything we experience loses meaning and we become disconnected from our own potential. "If you become bored, then you have to look at what excites you," sculptor John Pappas tells his students, "you have to find what you have a passion for—until then you keep experimenting." With passion life not only embraces meaning, it is infused with meaning. Alive in the frontiers of our passions, our lives manifest a continuum of new abilities and creative strivings.

Emerson said that everything in the universe goes by indirection. Meaning that there is no one straight way or course of action leading to the center of our creative and spiritual being. Yet underlying creative living, as well as many of life's creations, we find passion. We may experience it in different forms at different times but the fact still remains that our passions are forever connected to the workings of our life. One might sense it in the body as an excited need to commence a specific task. Mentally one my suddenly be flooded with images that appear understandably perceptive. Emotionally, the energies of passion can transform attachments; fears may contract, hopes may expand. Passions can also alter attitudes, taking us to other realms of freedom where shifts of imagination and identity are not only possible but occur as natural complements to our true nature.

Passions are doorways. When open, they allow us proper access to our spiritual journeys. If they are kept closed we cannot form a creative union with the world. Fulfillment in life is so closely connected to living creatively that without passion life would feel empty. To remain happily connected to the natural world we live in we need to live with passions illuminated by love. If our life is not full of love then there is room for hate. If life is closed to passions of spirit-filled love then it is open to anger and vulnerable bait to any number of perversions.

When it comes to the way one lives and ultimately

creates, unconscious power cannot be indiscriminately given to acting on impulse. Impulses are impersonal. Passions, on the other hand, are personally transcendent, going beyond levels of consciousness to become spiritual incarnations of the self. Our passion is relevant to expression and expression is foremost to creative living. If we don't honor our passions as an inherent part of our being, then an aesthetically sensitive and intimately close relationship to living will not be fully exposed to us.

Our passions are creatively expansive. By extending the limitless capacities of our spirit into actions, our passions dance with our expressions. The performance that ensues is always the most enjoyable part of life; there is more enjoyment to be found in the expression of an idea or feeling than there is in the mere thought of it. That's just the way it is. We create with our passions not with our mind. Our passions may empower our thinking but thoughts are only a minor excursion into the territory of creativity. Thinking resides on the dimensional plane of fact and reason not in the native realm of the senses. Its our passions that press us forward and offer us the flexibility to uncover new meanings in life; to appreciate new stimuli. Once we recognize this formative force of continuous energy and grasp its unsummoned possibilities we become more creative, and in our creativeness become more sensitive to the world around us. If our passions are alive in the face of life . . . our performance is never a solo dance.

Passions are common to us all. As both individuals and members of a shared community they are an evolutionary source of our achievements. Passions elevate us. We refer to them when assessing the details of our existence. We know we're living life close to our creative center whenever they are felt deeply. As a marvelous phenomenon of our spiritual destiny, passions ultimately initiate us into a creative freedom of being.

18

Generosity

C reativity is an act of generosity, a gift of the spirit. Generosity, as a primal and loving presence dwelling within every human being, has the potential to change every human experience. Creative human beings find little joy in possessing anything that goes unshared.

There is an ancient Chinese proverb that says, "To obtain happiness for one hour, take a nap. To obtain happiness for life, help others." As a teacher I can readily identify with the last part of this proverb.

A colleague of mine once remarked that I had probably made more potters than pots. While it is true that I have had thousands of ceramic students over the years, the fact still remains that I have made even more clay pieces, but the loving kindness of his remark has never gone unappreciated as many of my most exalted moments and rewarding accomplishments have occurred for me through teaching. Teaching is giving, and giving to another with what has been given to us is one of the greatest joys we can claim for ourselves in life.

At times life can be complex but generosity is not complicated. It lives in each of us naturally. Still, it needs to be nurtured. We enhance our chances of cultivating other perspectives on unselfishness when we recognize that happiness is not found in possessing as much as it is found in sharing.

Receiving is giving. A spiritual connection to wisdom is realized whenever we receive life with affection and have loving relationships with it in ways that allow for a caring desire to contribute to someone's or something's well being.

Teachers, like all creative people, discover a peaceful sense of well being whenever their creative gifts are shared. One of the roles I live in as a teacher is that of a permission giver. A big part of what I'm about in the studio-classroom setting is giving students the permission to be themselves. It may, at first, sound like a simple or insignificant purpose, when in fact it is an all-encompassing phenomenon with ripple-like consequences.

Self-knowledge is real knowledge. It disentangles the

strings of ignorance, fear, and greed removing them from a less than free sense of self. Knowing your self is the natural way to repeatedly access your creative capabilities in ever expanding ways. This connection between real self and creative self is not only a major spiritual truth but a creatively liberating one as well. The most direct means that I have for encouraging students to be themselves is the aura and freedom of my own being. Although I often try to talk about the mysteries of creative living, I still find that with most students learning becomes a spiritual state of essential associations. A state of heightened appreciation of the observed by the observer; a state of affection.

The more students become in touch with the breadth of their creative qualities the more their spirit reveals the nature of its unbounded connections. These connections unite them with all kinds of possibilities. They build relationships, generate wholeness and even produce new life. They can be creative, formative and even universal in nature but, inescapably, they remain spiritual. The human spirit is the glue that unites. It is the web that holds creative activity together, allowing it to emerge and evolve with some dimension of meaning.

At most, a compassionate teacher can lead us towards it, inspire us or provide a supporting place long enough for us to discover it. Yet it is each us who must ultimately be the guides to our own spiritual generosity.

Once discovered, however, generosity becomes our responsibility. For most of us that means gifting—being spontaneously generous in thoughts, words and deeds.

Gifting is an act of generosity. And, because it is often inspired by love, can be a natural, if not unconscious, expression of self. In true giving such as this, the gift itself no longer becomes the real gift. The gift here is more symbolic than physical and the true gift becomes the meaning.

In this type of giving the giver and the receiver are both gifted. For the receiver, taking now becomes a form of giving to the giver.

William Blake understood the universal miracle of giving when he wrote, "No bird soars too high if it soars with its own wings." Through the extended generosity of others we live. And in that living wonderful things occur to us, profound yet gentle things (some call them miracles) that enable us to recognize the truth of giving and, in turn, to become compassionate givers.

Giving also honors our spirit and brings it life. The best way to nurture your spirit is by giving. Taking is not a nurturing experience if it doesn't recognize the meaning of the gift or is not a cooperative part of the process. It would then become an experience made-up of unnatural feelings and anxieties. Taking is not the most natural feeling or trait of humanness. It is not a natural extension of our spiritual nature. Feelings of togetherness, sharing and love are. These are the real feelings of wholeness, they appeal to the caring spirit of who we are.

When we give, we are being creative. Giving is a bringing forth of our creative energies. It is nimble performance of our spiritual wholeness. Taking, on the other hand, that is not free of desire and wanting can be a fumbling display of undissolved selfishness; a quivering lack of self-knowledge that is heavily interlaced with seductive fragrances of ego.

The ego, here, is not only a predator that nips away at the body of our giving, it stalks it as well: seeing it as something to be prayed upon for sport and survival. There are many ways in which the ego attacks who we really are and keeps us away from our wholeness: our natural and loving self. When it comes to giving, the ego can be a major obstruction. Its desires can deafen and blind us to our own awakening by promoting the obligations of greed over the blessings of love.

Fortunately, our spirit embraces different motives. As with creativity, the motives of the spirit go far beyond the envelope of the ego and the smooth-talking logic of reason. The spirit is a dimension of love . . . it is forever alive in the self and flows with the actions of what we do. As receivers of our own spirit's gifts, we can, with gratitude, honor those gifts by wearing the true coat of our own generosity and, hopefully, unite with others and our world through giving.

The more one embraces generosity and lives a giving life the more one comes to realize that forgiveness is an archetypal creativity generator.

Forgiveness has virtually nothing to do with physically being creative. As with most spiritual gifts it too, is an indwelling perception. Yet without its healing properties the subconscious guilt of our many mistakes can keep us separated from our creative selves.

Forgiveness, most especially self-forgiveness, is perhaps the kindest and most profound example of generosity. Creative freedom is grounded in personal forgiveness. By forgiving yourself for all those past wrongs that have plagued you, you release your spirit from bondage; washing it clean and helping it to heal. Through the generosity of self-forgiveness the spirit acquires an abundance of new energy that can creatively be used by you to share your deepest self and to express your greatest truths.

Self-forgiveness is not selfishness. Self-forgiveness is a generous loving of self. It is allowing love to expand your life and your spirit to express itself more freely. Its all quite simple, when you are giving you are loving. Whatever the results, remain tolerant, your ahead, your honoring your spirit.

19

Intuition

Intuition is a natural faculty of comprehension. It is our simplest sense for knowing basic truths without having yet experienced them. It is knowledge ascertained through spirit; not through logic and reason. It is akin to that innate aspect of being, that instinctive knowing, that turned us to our mothers breast without yet knowing the hidden truth of its catering nourishment.

For the same reason that we don't look for the sun when the moon's out, we don't look for a rationale to justify such a self-sufficient quality of our humanness that is unseen yet known to be an important part of our wholeness.

Intuition is our hidden spiritual treasure. It is the inner image of our creativity. To discover it and to honor it is to recognize that we are both the mirror and the face in the mirror. We are spirit and what reflects spirit. When we embrace our spirit, not for purposes of examination but for guidance, we encircle our creativity and receive unexpected insights that echo deep from within.

There are few clues to the understanding of intuition. It is seemingly an enigma that cannot be solved, yet we are filled by its wisdom. Without knowing exactly why, it can suddenly transform us with a redeeming knowingness that is filled with both a purposeful function and an undisputed truth. How we surrender to it determines the streaming direction of our spirit and the strength of our creative flow. As the wisdom of our unconsciousness, intuition possesses more knowledge than our conscious mind can either comprehend or explain; what you choose to do with that information is what can open your spirit to my spirit or, for that matter, to anyone else's spirit. When such spiritual linking to the physical is experienced visually we call it art; when it appears as sound we call it music and so on. Although we seldom understand these inner forms, we respond to them and our forms generate other forms and vice-versa. If their existence thrives and influences other forms we call it art history, music history or whatever.

Artists instinctively know that their creative life is a reflection of some intimate connection between their spirit and intuition. The more transparent this connection appears, the more insightful they become at working and shaping the human materials of possibility. There is a power dwelling within the mystery of intuition that emanates an evolution of intelligences. A power that may be pre-human and that may go back to former animal, plant or mineral stages. The essentials of this innate force can and do direct a great deal of spirited creative activity. To watch ceramic sculptor Peter Voulkos tear, slash and spontaneously rearrange his clay into crude forms, that appear to be in an even greater state of havoc than the raw material he started out with, is to not only witness one the world's greatest ceramists at work, it is also the viewing of an animal-like sensibility alive with an energy inherited from a seemingly nonhuman realm. His creative work, his art, is one of the most honest, complete and successful extensions of a human spirit that I have seen. This man has a truly intimate relationship with the powers of his intuitive spirit. And his work is a radiant incarnation of that spirit.

I have often thought of abstract painter Helen Frankenthaler as someone who creates from an evolved state of intuitive awareness. Her uninhibited response to color and form is a deep honoring of intuition. Color and shape have no literal definition but her earlier paintings possessed an associative imagery that compositionally pulsed with scenic energy. Her later paintings, however, no longer suggest or invite this natural interpretation. They are more purely abstract, more compositional than composition and much less conscious than consciousness. They are begun with a "picture feeling" and are allowed to develop, in form and color, as the painting progresses. She acknowledges her vulnerability to being seduced by her talents but still prefers the uncertainty of unknown wonders to the known limits of what she can do. In essence, she seeks to find her colors and forms as she works rather than starting out with them.

For an artist to connect her self to the nature of her intuitive breadth, in order to give vitality to her paintings, she would also have to be connected to its value in day-to-day living. For the artist, art is ultimately an expression of self; of a reality that signifies self. In the same way that life is not a rational existence art is not a rational process. Art is not created rationally. Art is where the artist departs from reason and merges with the subconscious. To be creative the artist has to go beyond the known. Being creative is confronting the unknown, not as an intellectual expedition but as a spiritual traveler, and the adventure begins—comes to life—when homage is given to intuition.

Intuition becomes the guiding eyes of the creative traveler. Without preexisting models and plans to act as map and compass, new creative horizons are reached by the light of intuition. Moment by moment, its unseen presence carries the imagination to new, unique and creative vistas as its trusting vision sweeps aside obstacles of aimlessness and fear.

Each of us possesses a certain amount of fear when it comes to giving up some sense of conscious control to a process that is more instinctual than logical. American society and culture, historically, has promoted intellectual values and suppressed spiritual values. Even Freud frightened us away from encounters with our internal selves. Instead of professing passion for the creative spontaneity and universal love that dwells within us, he focused, all to often, on latent aggressive and destructive tendencies.

As an artist and as teacher, I have had to penetrate those inner realms, both in my self and my students, on countless occasions—sometimes very deeply. Instead of discovering dark demons, I have witnessed an expressive richness of possibilities and the embrace of visionary love. Without some form of intuitive connections to the spirit within us life can lose purpose. In other words, fear may be a natural presence but we should not allow it to expand into a toxic condition that threatens the evolution of our inner humanness and jeopardizes our sensory connections to life. To live creative lives we have to believe in our intuitive gifts; not fear them.

Intuitive gifts grow well in an environment of trust. Creativity requires its measure of faith, and intuition is a form of unstructured belief. It is frequently a new kind of truth connected to a different concept of intelligence. We might say that intuition is an intimacy with self that allows us to see beyond worldly appearances. As a voice from within, it exposes the objectified world we live in while, at the same time, portrays how that world exists in us.

Alive inside each of us are the sacred fires of individuality. As flames, invisibly fanned by the spirit, they seek to be discovered so that they can burn more brightly out in the open, casting new light across the terrain of our world.

On the path to our undiscovered worlds intuition is the warm light of dawn. We cannot undertake a creative journey without it. Our creative sense of self needs its mysterious guidance.

20

Communication

Communication is a revelation of spirit. It is the giving and the receiving of love. It is creation in action.

As a manifestation of our identity, it becomes our link to life. It can be the sharing of a tiny, barely visible, personal quality in the most intimate of settings or it can be an annunciation of grand magnitude. Whatever its scale, communication's purpose is to share, seek to understand and to grow. When is it required? Whenever we welcome our humanness and recognize our spiritual inspirations. It should occur instinctively, like the blinking of the eyes or unfold naturally like the morning's light.

Being creative and being communicative are intertwined. Each is the living edge of the other. You have to be both receptive and expressive for either one to balance out. It's similar to keeping your will and your desire going in the same direction. It keeps your feet from losing their balance.

Good communication touches more than the surface appearances of living. It goes beneath the simple veneers of sharing information and deepens feelings of fellowship. It enlivens relationships between individuals by uniting them in companionship and nourishing their union with the invisible love of the spirit. Communication that makes binding, life inspiring connections becomes a communion of love and has the capacity to bring great intimacy to the life of the spirit. When all involved are completely surrounded by the joy and tenderness of a meaningful exchange, feelings of separation fade and thoughtful appreciation emerges. For two friends this can become a symbolic point of departure. Communication that is mutually positive and activates intimacy can put into motion a series of events that heighten awareness and a new sense of truth.

When two lovers communicate, they have the potential to touch the very foundations of their individual being and with great feeling join their spirits so that it is in the world as one. They become a pure joy for everyone to behold. You see them; you see a portrait of *Love*.

Two such people are celebrating a beautiful union that could only have grown from a deep sharing of truth. In their communion with each other, they have learned to move with grace and confidence—sharing freely; holding nothing back. Their spirits, filled with love, overflow into each other leaving no room for doubt and unhappiness. Love for them is complete.

Love is the greatest gift of communion. Its compassionate awareness opens the door of possibilities between one's self and another human being. By communicating one can experience the spiritual closeness of love. And by knowing love one learns to live.

Loving, like creating, is communication. With every decision one makes to communicate through love a personal passageway to communion—to union—is opened. Being loving and being creative are two fundamental means for achieving communion: with ourselves, with others; with the world.

For the creative person activity is the portrait of communication. And this communication becomes a heroic portrait of self when it embraces the virtuous treasures of the human spirit. Self expression is a spiritual achievement; it is an act of personal freedom that is best recognized as a natural extension of identity rather than some phenomena of forced desires.

There are situations, unfortunately, where communication becomes over communication. A place where communication is forced and no longer appears easy or meaningful . . . where understanding is not understood and miscommunication occurs. These static and unconnected states can be very unnatural and frustrating. Not only can they destroy relationships, they are demotivating and deforming: limiting the activity of self expression. We yearn for healthy exchanges with others just as we yearn to express ourselves productively, but what is the right way? What is the right approach to making the right connections?

According to Marianne Williamson, "To communicate is to join and to attack is to separate." For a healthy exchange or positive bond to exist in any relationship loving and caring energies must be brought to it. Criticism and cynicism does not make for good communication. Unlike love, which heals relationships, negativity tears them apart.

Good communication is a sharing of spirit; poor communication ignores spirit. Communication, as a human tool of spirit, has always been an instrument for sharing. To transcend the barriers of noncommunication and begin open interactions with another we must first make the right connections within ourselves. Once we have achieved an honest dialogue with our spirit, with our authentic self, we are ready to communicate that self to the world—irregardless of the circumstances. If, however, we fail to establish a genuine form of communication with the sacred center of our spiritual self then whatever we communicate and express is a partial truth and we will be left to live with its consequences. Without being fully in touch with our spiritual self—our authentic self—I doubt whether we can authentically interact with others or express ourselves with any degree of authentic purpose and creativity.

The intrinsic laws of universal Karma always see to it that each of us gets what we've naturally earned and deserve. What this concept of balance implies, when applied to the subject of communication, is that each of us is going to be able to extend our external presence only to the extent that we penetrate our internal presence. In other words, the truth of our expression equals the truth of our identity . . . our communication, our communion, our union with self.

21

Mindfulness

Being creative is a choice we make with every breath we take. It's a moment-to-moment decision. It is mindfulness . . . a meaningful and compassionate connectedness with the details of our existence.

Mindlessness, on the other hand, is a blind reliance on a predetermined and fixed set of beliefs. It is an inflexible way of thinking and, as such, a chilling incarceration of creative thought, curiosity and discovery.

It is not uncommon for us to become desensitized to our life and overwhelmed with daily responsibilities that seemingly lead us away from instead of towards a peaceful and inspirational coexistence with living. Without a personal sense of peace and a feeling of inner happiness we are easily distracted from acting creatively. Lacking these deep feelings that a mindful understanding of life can so profoundly provide, we can easily become spiritually numb to the point where we are just alive enough to be creative voyeurs and little more, as there is little harmony of consciousness left for creative activism.

The deeper we go into the observance of life, of reality, the closer we come to liberating our creative spirit. As we learn and understand more about our personal lives, we are literally able to live them more creatively. Greater creative achievement, in most instances, is linked to our ability to focus awareness on those things we find to be personally meaningful. This is where enthusiasm becomes a great motivator. Since each of us has limited amounts of energy to commit to life's needs, the amount of attention we are able to allocate to those aspects of life we find interesting becomes critical to the cultivation of one's creative potential.

Creativity is bound to life and all of its evolutionary changes more than it is bound to established forms of truths. Being mindful is staying unattached to long-standing dogmas, theories or views of knowledge while remaining attached to the precious reality of one's own ever-changing truth. If you can find your way to question, comprehend and expand the experiences of life prior to accepting any of its boundaries, than you'll naturally recognize that being open to inquiry is a self-sustaining form of creativity that is more rewarding than clinging to any close-minded view.

The most complete source for our creative passions is an active and open mind. If, right now, we make ourselves available to consciously take in the effects that the circumstances of our life are making available to us ,we can catch hold of a reality that is our present: our life. In our expanded awareness of what is now our present reality we are better able to be creatively alive and active in the moment. By being attentive to the sounds, smells, and movements around us we become more alive to the rush of life. Try it! Right now. For starters, is there someone near you? A loved one, a close friend or maybe even a stranger? Stop and take the time to intimately look at them. What blessing are you touching for yourself, what compelling connections are being experienced? No one in sight? Okay, then take a closer look at this book. Tactically, how does it feel? Focus on experiencing just the feelings your fingers are capable of having by sensitively touching its overall form. Now, feel the smooth surface quality of the cover as compared to the rougher tooth of the text pages. What sounds do these pages make as you handle and turn them? Are there binding and paper smells? Take the time to let your mind relax and to feel the natural responses of all your senses. Visually, what is your response to the style and size of the type? The layout of the type, is it jammed together appearing psychologically unfriendly pushing you away or is it generously spaced and warm in its welcome, inviting you to join in and to become a part of its story? Ah! and my reading favorite, is there enough blank white space for the eyes to rest on?

These two brief exercises attempt to illustrate how we can extend rather than impede awareness. There are life issues of greater significance, but first we need to recognize the value in small things if we're to put forth an enlightened response.

Our awareness is what our life contains. Just like the pitcher pours what it contains, we express what we know. That's why mindfulness is so important: it is the self-stabilizing foundation of both our humanness and our expression. Without a knowledge and understanding of our life and all that we bring to it, we would easily lose ourselves. By not slowly observing and actively embracing the momentary details of our day-to-day life we are unable to live fully. Mindful living is meaningful living. It is living in the awareness of the actual moment and, immersed in our present whatever, we can find purpose, we can discover our uniqueness and we can give truth to our expression. What comes forth, ultimately, is the presence of our creativity and our ability to participate with it from a different perspective.

Creativity, in this context, is to be claimed internally;

not just attained externally. Our spirit is a host and home for our creativeness. It provides it with B & B (bed and board) while waiting for it to reveal itself in authentic and truthful ways, which may be a long time coming unless time is taken to consciously dwell within the present—the wholeness of each and ever emerging moment—with our full dimension of being. In short, the present is the only time in which our spirit can be alive. Just as we cannot claim our creativeness from a past time or commit it to a future time, our spirit can only be real for us in the present, because the only reality is the present.

It's often been said that the way we do one thing is the way we do everything. There is a great deal of truth to this saying because through the work we know the worker. What we do is always a portrait of who we are. This, every artist knows. Art, as an overflowing of one's creative self into the world, can touch many lives, but it also is a prodigious exposé of its creator. The attention we give to the details, those seemingly insignificant routines of life such as cleaning, waiting in line, walking, etc., become a noteworthy reflection of how and what we will bring to the rest of our life.

Creatively, we become very free when we recognize the potency of internal growth. As we learn to perceive the details of our existence, we find ourselves. When we open ourselves to life, we come to know ourselves. And, as we mindfully interact with the handling of the details of living our life, we become ourselves. Being our own self is the most important person we can be; it's an empowering position from which to make a difference in our behavior and the spiritual quality of our creativeness. Internal changes become major changes when they broaden the spectrum for creative expression and accomplishments. Such transcendent dimensions of consciousness reveal a seemingly natural runway to accommodate new flights of creative freedom.

III

LIVING LIFE CREATIVELY

22

Love: The Flowering of Self

There are several paths that we walk in life, but none is walked as often as the path leading toward a greater understanding of self. We walk this one repeatedly. It doesn't seem to matter how old we become or how many other paths we've traveled; career, romance, family, religion, health, wealth, adventure, etc., we always return to it.

The human drive to know self and to experience happiness is very, very strong. As we seek relevancy for our lives we begin to discover ways to live that are not as one-dimensional as they once were. As we begin to live more consciously, more attentively, our quest in life begins to focus on the inner self as the transforming source for fulfillment in life.

In my early twenties, I chose to travel the path of the artist. In many ways I became well-versed and successful in the world of art—primarily as a ceramist and secondarily as a designer and sculptor. While I was busy making things, building an exhibition record and adding to my resume I was losing sight of who I was and of why I even chose the artistic path in the first place. What happened was that I'd become preoccupied with doing *something* instead of being *someone*. With little thinking, and even less feeling, I had gotten into an unconscious habit of nourishing my career and ignoring my relationship with life. I had become dedicated to simply being an "artist" and not someone who embraced being an artist for the purpose it gave to my life.

Today I'm still very much the artist, only now art is a greater part of who I am and how I connect with my spiritual self and with life. On my many travels along that pathway to self, I found that love was the multi-dimensional force of change in my world. It became the source of my awakening. It became a force that could work miracles. Today I create art because I literally love to do so, and I do it with love. No longer does what I do separate me from my spirit—from who I am.

In our humanness we have a primal need to love and to be loved. Whenever love bursts forth in our lives, like a flower in all its colorful magnificence, we glow with delight and experience all sorts of feelings, especially those of unity, joy and peace. When we create with love we not only transform our own spirits but also those around us. With love we make connections to all of creation.

Almost any ordinary connection to life is a revealing visit with truth when it is grounded in love. As a basis for spiritual discovery, the connections that we need to make with our inner selves are the most consequential ones. They have an inspirational effect on one's spiritual qualities. If we cannot connect with our own self we will be unable to make contact with our spirit. The cycle is that simple, and if we're unable to touch our own spirit we most certainly will be unable to associate with our creative energies.

The vast empty space, as it were, that keeps us isolated from our own identity can be transversed. No matter how treacherous the terrain, or how long the journey leading to self-discovery, the wilderness that separates us from our own spirit is that place within us that is estranged from love. All of us have those internal spaces of self that we've ventured into, like strangers into a foreign land, and wandered around in half lost, half confused. Yet it is us that makes them lonely, impersonal spaces.

If we're the source of our own disconnections, then we become responsible for making the changes that bring us to wholeness. Anaïs Nin once said that there came a time in her life when the risk to remain tight in a bud was more painful than the risk it took to blossom. For us to blossom we have to penetrate all of our empty spaces and fill them with purpose and meaning—with love.

Each of us have to initiate the changes that allow for a new emergence of self. With love as our transport we will always be taken in the right direction and brought to the center of our learning: to love ourselves.

Your love is your why and wherefore in life. It is finding yourself and sharing yourself. It is embracing life and it is caring for life. It is enjoying all of creation and it is being creative.

Robert Morley understood a crucial truth for avoiding an unlived life when he said that the first secret of happiness was to fall in love with yourself. Loving one's self should not be associated with feelings of self-centered guilt. Love of self is fundamental to living a full life. If, for example, we are unable to love ourselves, we will be unable to love others. And, it might be added, others would find it difficult to love us. Love begets love. If any guilt were to be found, pertaining to myths of self-love, it should be placed in those areas where the self is continuously sacrificed, ignored or denied for the happiness of others. This devalues love, devalues self. Without a love of self we would be unable to bring creative leadership to our lives.

23

Giving Way To Love

To understand love as an energy rather than simply as a romantic emotion is to know the depths of creative possibilities. As energy, love is the foundation of creativity.

Within the context of human creativity we should remain mindful of the two primary emotions through which we endlessly operate upon: love and fear. One is real, the other is not real. With each and every experience in life we have a choice of responding to the encounter with either one of these two physiologically charged sensibilities, one of which is continually creative and the other ultimately destructive.

Loving energy is primal energy grounded in wholeness. Our humanness is its center and our humanness, like our love, is not physical matter but an ongoing form of energy. As energy our love has eternal characteristics. Its existence can be infinite and its ability to host loving and creative responses, long after we are no longer physically present, is almost without end. Fear, on the other hand, has no such evolutionary lifeline. Because it is reactivly centered in what is around us, rather than within the threshold of our human wholeness, it has no faithful following; no natural permanence.

Fear is a response that our ego, as a reflection of external circumstance, presents to us. The ego may dress-up the look of fear so that it is portrayed in a less threatening form such as tradition, habit, science, dogma, rational, progress or any number of images that, on the surface, look appealing yet exist as hidden roots entangled in toxic soil. Through judgment the ego opens the door even further for fear, and although love is above fear, judgment infuses fear with self-righteous credibility.

The ego has long been associated with our creative empowerment. When, in fact, the ego is a projection of our perception of the creative energies of others. Our ego does not project who we are as much as it projects who we think we should be. Ego does not represent our creative self, spirit does. Spirit is not only the interpreter of our internal self, it is our creative energy and a natural manifestation of self. Ego, although often present, is an unnatural characteristic of self. Where ego is a representative of external interests, the spirit is a representative of our real self.

To know the spirit as a liberating force we need to understand the origins of unsound ego feelings in order to move beyond them. Our spirit is our creative center, our creative strength. Our spirit, not our ego, provides us with unlimited opportunities for living creatively.

Mother Teresa said, "If you judge others then you are not giving love." What she is suggesting, I think, is that continuous evaluation and judgments block the natural flow of the spirit and restrict creative energies from more meaningful pursuits.

Judgment is more a matter of ego than wisdom. It competes for discovery and contradicts the energy the spirit provides. To become non-judgmental is to broaden one's character and allow greater access to the energy sources that love evokes. Our need to judge is diminished whenever our need to give way to love is spiritually realized as having a larger purpose and authentic value.

Learning to live a life grounded in love's energy is the greatest spiritual gift one could hope for. With love we are able to form a responsive bond with all of our other spiritual gifts. Our love is what creatively connects us to life and allows us to live more harmoniously through its changes and mysteries. Love is what matters. Without its connection life would become meaningless. It would lack the quality and value that love so naturally provides.

Sometimes it is useful to slow down, to take time out and to contemplate the actions we have put our love into. One guidance exercise for understanding how we let the spirit of love move through us involves memory and meditation. Sitting quietly in a place of comfort, search your memory for one or two genuinely loving things that you have recently done in your life. They can be quite modest, simple and plain. Now, as you picture them, meditate on how they have affected you . . . did these experiences open your heart further? I. M. Pei believes that good architecture lets nature and light in. Did your love let awareness in?

Awareness is a powerfully creative tool. It increases options by offering new opportunities for change. Whenever we expand our awareness we expand our vision by reducing our fears and the limitations of our experience. Which is why, creatively, there is no external change that isn't first proceeded by an internal change. According to Carlos Castaneda things don't change, we change our way of looking . . . that's all.

One of the roles that love plays in the creative process is that it focuses our attention—providing it with a value that is both spiritual and meaningful. Whenever an element of love is involved in a creative undertaking the end result becomes more purposeful and the results, I might add, more far reaching and long lasting. Its as if love is the archival ingredient. Any aspect of creativity that embraces it becomes empowered; that which doesn't lacks personal relevance, encompasses failure and invites defeat. Love is not a thing, it's not objective. It is subjective and therefore universally integrated so that things created or inspired with it, whether they be objects of art, relationships or forms of government, can realize enormous returns. If you recognize love as the face of our spirit, you can easily imagine how, for example, a government, infused with its spirit, can mirror that spirit in any number of ways.

Creativity is the love that lives within us; the greater the love the greater the possibilities. As with love, the same is true for all of the treasures of the spirit. Each and every one of them play key leadership roles in the advancement of our creative consciousness and behavior.

The more we come to embody these gifts and treasures of our spirit, the closer we come to understanding one of the primal truths of human creativity: that who we are is the unfolding center of all creative energy. The visible/external manifestations that we call art, invention, vision, enlightenment or whatever, are the children, not the parents, of this invisible internal energy.

There are many fundamental aspects to loving, just as there are to a knowledge of self, that are difficult to perceive if one doesn't proceed to connect with their capacities and give them expression. Love has to be communicated, expressed and shared to permeate life. If you could not immediately acknowledge some act of loving kindness or virtuous undertaking during the previous exercise it would not, in any way, imply that you had moved through your life without loving. It may simply imply that you are less than open with yourself in realizing just how much love resides within you. It might also indicate a need for letting go, of becoming free of life's restraints, including judgments, and undertaking a different path. One that is touched by the spirit and where love is capable of flowing through you.

As the ultimate gift of the spirit, love serves to connect us with other spiritual treasures in ways that bless our life and bring it great peace, and, as a creative force, love is what allows us to live our life fully. If you have something you love to do or love someone who loves you, for example, you have a precious essential for happiness. When such love is lacking, life experiences are less grounded in the wisdom of compassion. No love no joy. Similarly a life without love is not alive with an energy of freedom or the sustained peace of liberation that follows in its path.

Love is so powerful—so extraordinarily important—that without it our spiritual life cannot become fully integrated with our creative life. For this integration to occur, every aspect of our life must embody love. This one simple, yet universal, truth affects everything in our lives and the lives of those around us.

Much of the unhappiness in life arises from a lack of love. According to Dr. Deepak Chopra, a brilliant and insightful teacher, unhappiness results from identifying with one's self-image rather than one's higher or natural self: a self that is genuinely loving. In his book *The Path to Love* he reminds us that, "When you truly find love, you find yourself." Like spirit and creativity, love and self are so similar, so interrelated, that to access one is to access the other. In fact, to the degree that we nurture any one of these four realms we simultaneously nurture the other three.

Love is a verb. What matters in everyday life, is that our path is one with love and that our every movement along the way is motivated by love. Emerson begins his essay on *Love* by writing, "Every soul is a celestial Venus to every other soul." Through love, we deeply touch others and are deeply touched by them. This is happiness and, in a spiritual sense, the sacredness in life.

I'm especially found of one approach Deepak Chopra

suggests for putting love into action. He calls it the *Law of Giving*. It consists of giving something to everyone we make contact with. The giving mentioned, I'm sure, is a feeling gift of self. It could take a material form like baked cookies or wild flowers, but he had something more powerful in mind. In *The Seven Spiritual Laws of Success*, Chopra tells us, "The gifts of caring, attention, affection, appreciation and love are some of the most precious gifts you can give."

The pathways to living creatively are accessed through love and not fear. A creative life is not characterized by fear. It is not afraid of what others think. It does not pay homage to what others value unless it recognizes those values as a part of its own uniqueness. A creative life does, however, honor its own objectives; adapts to its own beliefs.

To live creatively one has to think their own thoughts, live their own dreams and follow their own conscience, not out of fear and compromise but out of a love for one's own integrity and the freedom to nourish one's own happiness.

In so many ways, creativity is love. You have often heard it said, that "love works miracles". That's because its presence penetrates everything and, as an invisible force, eliminates many obstacles that stand in the way of a collective uniting and the completion of expressive communication. Life with love is an existence without separation. There is a mindful sense of togetherness, of a connectedness to a greater reality, when one is feeling the transformational energies of its timeless sovereignty. It is such a major cornerstone to a creative life that it would be hopeless to even make attempts at being creative without being loving. Love is a natural foundation for creative growth. If your spirit is not open to love, of self as well as life, then being creative from your deepest, best and most sensitive places becomes unachievable.

If our creative accomplishments are not fused with love the circumstances surrounding their survival, influence or what have you, become significantly weakened. Creative undertakings that begin as extensions of our being posses the greatest potential to touch others and bestow long lasting results. Whenever we dedicate the deepest strengths of our creative being—our love—to an activity we endow it with profound value.

Creative expressions conceived in the spirit of love are not only endowed with genuine value, they are consigned to live with grace and serve with meaning. As human beings with a purpose in life, if indeed one believes that we are born with any such responsibilities, that purpose would be, I'm convinced, to share love. What's life about, if not to give and receive love? We can do a lot with our lives, from building bank accounts to building empires, but if what we do is not rooted in love then not only do the great things become insignificant but the little ones, too.

All too often the importance of love goes unrecognized until something dramatic or traumatic happens. Elisabeth Kübler-Ross, a psychiatrist who has interviewed thousands of people that have had near-death experiences, identifies four phases of life following death. The third phase, after experiences of leaving the physical body and entering a state of spirit energy, is the one that she claims reveals the meaning of life, which is love.

It seems that nearly everyone who survives a near-death experience becomes a changed person. Major shifts in values are reported to have occurred. Material things become unimportant. What one does becomes important. Loving becomes the primal expression. It enters as the shared connection between self and another: a truthful communion with humanity. It participates in letting us know what life is about.

What's of most interest here is the revelation that a large number of individuals return with feelings of unconditional love. Hopefully a crisis, such as an encounter with death, is not needed to awaken us to the wisdom of loving—to the real source of creative power. Each of us has the ability to journey forth and find its divine initiative. Along the way, however, we must repeatedly soften ourselves to its touches, as we continually need to prepare for the wholeness of our human-ness. With our life we touch others but with our love we can touch them, and life, in ways that are significant and worthwhile.

If we cannot open ourselves to love then we cannot become open to our own gifts. If we're unable to access our spiritual nature we will be unable to have a creative relationship with life. Creatively, love matters. With love we can touch those places deep inside that give us the clarity to not only seek the right questions but to find the right answers to life's design. By living and creating in these questions, in these answers, we discover life's purpose.

24

Spiritual Unfolding

The wholeness of the spirit, like the wholeness of many things, is comprised of segments which are, in themselves, complete entities. While there are many "whole-segments" that make up the composite presence of spirit, at no time is its wholeness ever revealed to us. At best, we can only comprehend segments and sub-segments, but even in our ignorance these segments still can appear to be awesome. Love, for example, is just one segment—one treasure of the spirit—yet it is undoubtedly the highest achievement that humans aspire to experience and even if they find their deepest fulfillment through love, there are latent aspects of its existence that remain hidden. Still, within the mystery of the not knowing, there is clarity; a presence of love's wholeness. Sometimes, just to have a feeling for love's possibilities is to live in the divine majesty of its existence.

Creativity and the health of the spirit go hand-in-hand. Whenever any of these "whole-segments" that constitute spirit cease to evolve or mature they subvert the development of other "whole-segments". If left to flounder in a state of distress they eventually degenerate and impair spiritual growth by instigating a series of internal skirmishes that divert resources normally used for growth energy into defensive energy. Without even realizing it, we employ a lot of our positive spiritual energy toward improving, resolving and casting-off any number of repressively neurotic disorders that generate negative effects. The more time and activity we have to employ in emancipating these unevolved aspects of self and liberating them from our ignorance the less time we have to explore the higher revelations of our unknown potential.

The greatest tragedy in life, according to Thomas Carlyle, is not so much what men suffer, but rather what they miss. If, in our day-to-day living, we keep the presence of our spirit locked-up inside our chest how will we ever learn to appreciate it, yet alone be affected by it? Artist Robert Motherwell believed that art's content was based on feelings and that the artist's role was to create through and for sensing. As an artist, Motherwell's intense feelings provided a great deal of energy to his artistic activity. He was constantly striving to unlock the complex spiritual qualities of his own being so that his canvases could reflect feelings that the world might not otherwise know. He believed, for example, that if Cézanne had failed to penetrate some essential aspect of his spirit that individually unique feelings, resulting from the compositional elements in his paintings, would be lost to the world.

Some people aren't consciously oriented to the functions of their internal dimensions. They are intensely dissociated from a heartfelt perspective of their human potential. Isolated from their spiritual center, their psychological capacities, their emotional matrix, etc. they basically remain hostage to external influences, where ego-centered needs render them incapable of differentiating, yet alone integrating, their internal self with their external identity. These same individuals, for example, would only enter the interiors of architecture with their bodies or paintings with their eyes when they could also enter with their spirit and make it a truly significant experience. The spirit is the primal unifier. It is the connecting force. The spirit links the interior with the exterior and points the way to wholeness.

Approached developmentally as an evolution of consciousness, our identity as a physical and mental self becomes an identity with a spiritual self. With the achievement of spiritual identity the possibilities for creative imagining are miraculously increased. Creative movements, once housed within confined perceptions of self, find new openings to greater freedom.

The spirit is the atmosphere in which all good feelings blossom. The spirit opens the gate between identity and creativity and unites them in its image. It brings you to a new path marked with feeling. You identify with a new identity. You identify with your real self and not with a projected image of self. It's like going to the Grand Canyon instead of looking at a photograph of the Grand Canyon. There is no longer room for an identity crisis only for an identity manifest. You become you! And you create with a spirit that expresses itself through every dimension it possesses.

In this formative process, spirituality is an intimate shift from the external to the internal and then, with identity transcendence, back again. Only now the shift is from a self-centered to a universe-centered identity. An identity with a conscious awareness of one's intrinsic connections to everything living.

This state of our consciousness becomes genuinely spiritual when understanding is integrated with compassion for all that is life and, in certain instances, values it even more than our own.

Through the treasures of the spirit our creative identity and thinking is expanded beyond the limiting boundaries of self-centered performance options and presented with wider possibilities that are more universal in their resolve and vision. Such expansiveness is a natural essence of creativity and gets to the source of our living. It takes us to the sensation of our spirit and places beyond our knowing. Creativity, like works of great art, music, or dance, affirms that life is not without meaning and that being human is what makes it worth living.

Once we recognize the dimensions of the spirit we can identify with its natural role in our evolution as loving and creative beings. As we live with its energy, our identity as a physical-mental self becomes an identity with a spiritual self. When we experience the expansive domains of spiritual awareness, we embrace the very heart of our creativity. Suddenly we begin to mesh, we merge and we become one with this life-gifting force. In essence, we become a totally creative being. Consequently, with our identity no longer alienated from our spirit, we discover that creativity is every bit a function of spirit as it is of material or activity. When I make pottery, for example, I don't doubt for a second that my spirit, not my hands, is the real force that creatively shapes my clay.

Self is spirit, creativity is spirit acknowledged. Of all that we are, it is ultimately our spirit that leads us to our creativity and guides our humanness past existing limitations.

It should come as no surprise to suddenly discover that ones spiritual identity and creative center is directly connected to the spiritual universe of humanity's creative center. With the emergence of one's creative identity one merges with a collective identity. With similar understandings that significantly affect knowledge and experience the world over, creative people naturally share a mutual love for all living things, which goes far beyond just identifying with and caring about all human beings. A creative identity is an expanded identity. It is also a compassionate identity in that it feels rather than calculates its way to the right and creative resolution to every need. It is one that could not, for example, take the life of an animal for sport. As a lovingly creative being you are one with all of creation and creation is now deeply seen as being one with you. In other words, you are that animal.

When you encounter your creative center, your spiritual humanness, you go from a state of individual independence to one of collective interdependence. Your interconnectedness to all that is life is revealed with such a blessedness that you are able to see that animal as you see yourself. Even more importantly, you'll realize that the way you react towards the animal you react towards yourself. We are so interconnected to our world that we ultimately have to rely on each others support for survival. Spiritually, our interrelationship to everything we encounter can either imprison us or release us. Creatively, we can just as easily discover ourselves as lose ourselves in any of our actions.

The leap one makes to become a creative being is a big one. Without the treasures of the spirit we could not go the full distance needed to make such a leap and thereby make a creative difference with our life. Creation, unlike destruction, is generated by caring. Creation finds its greatest meaning within the most expansive yet innocently simple experiences of caring, a caring that exists as a shared crystallization of humanity's best virtues and collective dreams.

In caring, one can often give more than is expected. A spiritually healthy aspect of caring is that it opens our heart and enables us to attach something positive to everything we do. By always doing something positive we bring spirit to our activity and creativity to our life. We never sacrifice the health of our being when we are true to our spirit . . . true to ourselves. Caring reveals our innermost creative genius, not caring conceals it. By being honest with ourselves we learn to care and to enjoy the truth of our spiritual growth. Remember, where there is caring there is vision and our vision is what makes us a creative person.

It is not difficult to develop a creative attitude; a spiritually healthy life. If life is accepted as it is, and for what it is, one simply has to help make it better. The starting place for that voluntary undertaking is where you are now. By being open to your own personal gifts (a dream, a mood, a thought or even a laugh) one or more of them can become that centered place that changes your life for the better. Such a place is just not one of destiny, it is a place of choice. A place of possibility that allows you to go within yourself and find the starting point that both motivates and celebrates your unique resources and allows you not only to perform creatively but magnificently!

25

Creative Coalescence

One could endlessly wrestle with assumptions of what defines life's horizons or one could cut to the heart of the subject and embrace every moment of its existence.

The point here is that life is to be lived . . . not simply survived but really lived. We can truly honor our living by unlocking our creativity. Every moment of every day we have a choice as to how we will greet life. With those choices we can have a creative impact on our existence. We can broaden horizons until we come to a place of spiritual peace and to a place of freedom that allows us to make a difference: not just for ourselves but for the world. This we owe to ourselves—to the blessing of our life.

It is up to each of us to own our actions and to create our own lives. Spiritually it is always more constructive to refrain from saying or doing things that promote division, cause harm or create conflict. Such actions only serve to destroy our overall peace. Humanly, it is easy to blame, to deny or even to lie but it is equally as easy to be positive and to turn fears into hope and to allow that hope to motivate change.

The majority of life's obstacles come from within but if we utilize the nourishing strengths of our spiritual treasures we are liberated: we are shown the wisdom of our inner life. Aware of our inner presence, we can go about living within the world while simultaneously living within our spiritual nature. In the same way that a facial expression is fifty percent of communication or attitude seventy five percent of success, our spirit is a big percentage of our knowing. It is an inner doorway to knowledge. Knowledge based upon spiritual understanding becomes internally valuable to creative living. Since it is not the result of external norms, opinions and habits it becomes a self-reliant source by which we obtain the independence to take charge of our own life and to transcend living as a day-to-day exertion of survival. Such knowledge is an internal force that is centered around the spirit and focused on values. It brings meaning to what may have been meaningless. Knowledge based upon spiritual understanding does not confuse effort with results; it creates opportunities and identifies activity with creativity.

Our capacity for creativity is, at times, unimaginable. Children have it in great abundance. What happened to us when we grew up? Were our creative beginnings all an illusion? I don't think so, but however we see our past, the present, the now, is all that there is and the reality of the now is that it gives each of us a clean slate. With every new moment we receive a new invitation from life, a new opportunity for a new beginning. Left without our yesterdays, will we choose to take on the present—our now—with an open spirit full of creative possibilities? The deeper question is, and always should be, are you ready to shed the past and to greet new life with an enlightened spirit?

There are many ways to view life. A sea journey is one of those ways. If, sometime in the future, you want to sail a creative course on the waters of life your going to need a boat . . . and the better the boat the better the journey.

I like to think of the boat that I'm sailing as being well built: beautifully crafted yet designed to withstand strong winds and rough waves. I also think of my boat as representing various gifts of my spirit. The hull, for example, symbolizes values. And, like everyone's values, mine too remain below the surface, partially hidden from view, yet a buoyant support to my existence. Just to be afloat in the ocean of life is cause enough for celebration but to also feel its every motion as we celebrate it makes that gift our blessing.

You might diagram the various other parts of your boat differently, but I see the keel of mine as being integrity. Just as a keel can prevent a boat from capsizing, integrity is a stabilizing force in life. It keeps one upright while at the same time reducing sideways drifting. The mast is love—nothing else provides as much strength. The rudder is intuition. Jonas Salk once said that, intuition tells the thinking mind where to look next. Ancient sailors navigated by it, even after they learned to follow the stars. When the night time skies cloud over only intuition stays.

Our creative journey begins when we raise our sails to catch the wind. The spirit, of course, is the sail of the boat. In the same way that creativity is a quality of being that is the result of spirituality, and not the other way around, the sail (the spirit) is what moves the boat: the boat does not move the sail. If we don't care for our sails or use them properly we're unable to catch the winds of change and savor the exhilaration of authentic movement that brings us face-to-face with our real course in life.

As the captain of your ship, who you are becomes the

focus of the journey. You become responsible for charting a course through life's waters that can lead you to a creative existence. By tacking, and than tacking again, the course can be stayed. During squalls of activity or times of drift, when the winds of opportunity are lacking, a supportive crew made up of family and friends are a great help. Guided by their support and the multi-directional gifts of the spirit as a compass, one is always able to sail on. Just as the reading on this compass will differ as you turn to various courses of action, the needle itself will always turn to the same direction: allowing you to maintain your spiritual centeredness. Nothing is insignificant that pertains to the gifts of the spirit. The spirit, quite literally, is the compass of life. The longer you use its gifts to navigate and explore the waters of life, the more you'll discover about your natural identity: a discovery of existence that can cultivate a real trust in your own purpose and creative abilities.

Art is an expression of creativity and the direction of our creative journey is a natural progression. Remember, each creative act is an excursion of the spirit; a journey into the treasures of your spirit and personal views of life. Whenever we create something new we transform our physical world but, our world does not have to change for us to become creative, only our perception of it needs to change.

We live a more creative life, and become the caretakers of our future, when we awaken to new perceptions of life. Our behavior becomes more creative when we perceive life with a broader perspective. Which is creatively empowering. Our perceptions of ourselves and of the experiences in our lives direct our actions. If we see our lives as flourishing our expressive behavior will naturally be a positive representation of those feelings. Likewise, in the midst of feelings of insignificance, we're more likely to be swept-up in negative fears and avoid the taking of risks. It's not always easy to conquer those fears but if we can relinquish judgments and invite new beginnings, we can access the interior pathways of our creative potential. And, like an awakening, something deeply powerful happens, in that we don't withdraw from the experience, we give ourselves freely to it.

Creative power is one of the spiritual treasures that we have within each of us. It is not an external gift. The invisible dimensions of our inner creative resources are without restrictions. All that is needed for their outpouring are perceptions surrounded in the higher energy of the spirit and the wisdom of its humility. This release need not be a hard struggle for liberation but rather one of a soft surrendering.

Life, like love, opens to us when we open to it. Whenever we love we amplify our capacities to live a greater life. Whenever we trust we are in a position to unlock the doors to a larger reality. If we recognize that the world smiles when we smile, loves when we love, then we have a clearer perception of how to give new purpose and possibility to everything in life.

To gain a more intimate understanding of creativity as a spiritual manifestation of love it might help to see ourselves not as humans attempting to live creative lives but creative beings striving to live more humanly.

"It is something to be able to paint a particular picture, or to carve a statue, and so to make a few objects beautiful", Henry David Thoreau once wrote, "but it is far more glorious to carve and paint the very atmosphere and medium through which we look, which morally we can do." In looking back at my life as a visual artist, a maker of objects, I can see how, for years, I was overcome with the zeal of being a professional "artist" instead of simply being an authentic one. For a long time I had given my heart and soul into what I did technically and was made weary from the endless doing. Making art is a demanding venture. Limitless options and unexpected needs require more than an ordinary amount of discipline and sacrifice. Making art with spiritual purpose and personal meaning can easily get lost in the excitement of art as an activity. Generally it takes an artist a long while before they figure out that being someone who shares their spirit with life itself embraces just as much joy as being a creator of things.

If we are "to carve and paint the very atmosphere" of

our life in the way Thoreau was referring to, we have to recognize the role of the spirit in leading us to our creative gifts. Each of us is a part of creation, a part of some higher universal order, yet it remains for each of us to make the space in our lives for our unique spirit to emerge: for you to become you and for me to become me—for individual wholeness to occur.

Our time for wholeness is now at hand. It is our time to put down this book and pick-up our lives again. Both the writing and reading of these pages are about to reach an end. And we're about to part ways. Having taken a longer than brief hiatus from art making, I am now more than ever motivated to to totally immerse myself into the creative process, my sacred process, of doing what I love to do most and that is to make art. More specifically, to make ceramic sculpture. It is my creative work, my spirited work; my most sacred expression of me.

Through these pages we have looked at the tips, and believe me when I refer to them only as tips, of the creative and spiritual icebergs. Having written about them I am now ready to explore them to even greater depths by putting myself into creative action. After reading about them my hope is that you, too, are inspired into creative action. Not in the usual or conventional ways but in new and personal ones.

Now is our time to let go, to unthink, to feel, to trust

and to be ourselves. To be our creative selves, our genuine selves. The artwork that I make, as soon as this manuscript is put to press, will be as fresh, as free, as creative and as real a part of me as anything I have yet made. As I now become more alive and daring with my life what are you going to do? What are you going to do with the realizations that have been aroused within you through these pages? How are you going to live a more creative life? A more self-expressing and self-fulfilling life? And, yes, a more successful life.

Success, you know, is not all that difficult to achieve if you just direct and commit your imagination and creative energies to doing what you most want and enjoy doing or, in other words, by being, in the most simplest of senses, who you really are. Do you want to be successful at something or with something? Then do so . . . now is the time to get on with it.

What do you want to achieve? Do you want successes in the art world? In the financial world? In a love relationship, with gardening, or in cooking? You fill in the blanks. Go to the spirit of who you are and be you. Not just to be a successful somebody at something but, more than any one thing, to be you. To live and be you. In time, one can almost guarantee that you will succeed at being successful; not only because you wanted the achievement but because you chose to be creative—you became you!

Warren Buffett, an American folk hero, is the financial worlds most successful stock investor. As a self-made multi-billionaire, he created his successes in the marketplace not by listening to a herd of market professionals, but by being his own person and also, in his own words, a "realist". Buffett is a man of patience, character and little self-doubt. And, like his mentor Ben Graham, appears to be less interested in the accumulation of wealth than in the creative challenges of sound investing. The success of his investment strategy as a long term buyer of values is solely based upon what he personally believes to be the right thing to do depending on his perception of a company's value and not on investment theories, economic factors and market value. He is a creative analyst, a realization of self, who looks in the mirror if he needs to look anywhere for guidance.

In reality, being creative is little more than being who you are—being your real self. It is not a fantasy attempt to adopt the filtered behavior or perceptions of others. It is not being someone else. In *Hamlet*, one of the greatest plays ever written, we hear Polonius say to Laertes, "This above all: to thine own self be true." If one is not true to their real self; does not know or accept who they are, their capacity for thinking creatively becomes less than adequate. Lacking a conscious understanding of the various aspects of self that constitute the unique kaleidoscope of identity, one is prevented from relating them to one another and from activating the wholeness of self within the functional phase of creativity: which is, putting it all into action.

The inspiring teacher and painter Robert Henri understood, like Warren Buffett, that personal success was ultimately found in the creative work itself and not beyond it. Henri's paintings hang in Washington's National Gallery and New York's Metropolitan Museum yet he found his personal wisdom and happiness in the spirit of the doing. For him, the human activity of doing creative work, and doing it well, was what brought balance to life and beauty to the world. To Henri it didn't matter if one worked as an artist or not, what mattered was the doing itself and, that it be done well. As with everything both you and I choose to do, it is the quality of our being that we bring to the effort that gives it value and opens possibilities.

Life, itself, is a creative encounter. As you face it, you greet yourself. As you interact with it you engage yourself and, in this simple yet miraculous process, you have the ability to find your true essence. With the wisdom from knowing the treasures of your own spirit, go into the world and live a creative life that you can find fulfilling. Rejoice in what you do. For to live the life of a creator is a great benefit to others and an even greater kindness to yourself.

The writing of these pages has been an important learning experience for me. They are a personal part of my own journey and are shared in a spirit of love. My hope is that they also help you to treasure your spirit and to expand its creative accomplishments. What has been communicated between us has occurred from spirit to spirit and as a final exchange from my spirit to your spirit I leave you with 12 simple signs of spirit wisdom to ponder on.

12 Signs of Spirit Wisdom

A shifting of trust to internal instincts & intuition

An appealing sense of personal lightness

Feelings of inner clarity & freedom

A sense of being at home almost anywhere

Repeated occurrences of gratitude & generosity

A persistent presence of Spirit everywhere

Desires to contribute to the common good

Heightened sensitivity

Greater sense of humor

Unconditional caring

Rapid acceptance of change

Increased creativity

General References

The books listed below have been important developmental resources for my research into the nature of this publication. They were especially helpful in establishing some key motifs for the opening and closing chapters.

De Angelis, Barbara. *Real Moments*. New York: Dell, 1994.

Karpinski, Gloria D.. *Where Two Worlds Touch*. New York: Ballantine, 1990.

Kornfield, Jack. *A Path With Heart*. New York: Bantam Books, 1993.

Moore, Thomas. *Care of the Soul*. New York: Harper-Collins, 1992.

Richards, M.C.. *Opening Our Moral Eye*. New York: Lindisfarne Press, 1996.

Wilber, Ken. *A Brief History of Everything*. Boston: Shambhala, 1996.

Notes

21. Sinclair, William. *Selections From The Writings Of John Ruskin*. Edinburgh: W. P. Nimmo, Hay, & Mitchell. p. 434.

22. Beals, Carleton. "Background of Bigotry." *Catholic Digest* August 1960: p. 102.

24. Stiles, Kristine, and Peter Selz. *Theories and Documents of Contemporary Art*. California: University of California Press, 1996. pp. 25–26.

24. Barnstone, Willis. *The Other Bible*. New York: HarperSanFrancisco, 1984. (70) p. 305.

25. ———. *The Other Bible*. New York: HarperSanFrancisco, 1984. (112) p. 307.

37. Cameron, Julia. *The Vein of Gold*. New York: Tarcher/Putnam, 1996. p. 331.

44. Mueller, Tom. "The Naples Renaissance: An Interview With Antonio Bassolino." *Hemispheres* July 1997: pp. 24–28.

58. Bray, Anna J. "Poet Laureate Robert Pinsky: Using the Arts As A Tool For Learning How To Think." *Investor's Business Daily* 14 July 1997: A1+.

67. Ackrill, J. L. *Aristotle's Ethics*. London: Faber & Faber, 1973. (1177b33–1178a2) p. 174.

68. Elderfield, John. "Leaving Ocean Park" *The Art of Richard Diebenkorn*. New York: Whitney Museum of

American Art / University of California Press, 1997. p. 115.

77. *Dead Poets Society*. Dir. Peter Weir. With Robin Williams. Touchstone Pictures, 1989.

80. Kennedy, John F. *Profiles in Courage*—Commemorative Edition. New York: Harper Perennial, 1964. pp. 132–158.

83. Milton, John. *Paradise Lost*. New York: Odyssey Press, 1935. Book 1, line 254, p. 17.

85. Swindoll, Charles R.. *Man to Man*. Michigan: Zondervan Publishing House, 1966. p.63.

89. Nin, Anaïs. *The Diary of Anaïs Nin Volume Four 1944–1947*. New York: Harcourt Brace Jovanovich, 1971. p. 67.

92. Neret, Gilles. *Matisse*. Koln: Taschen, 1996. p. 19.

93. Pappas, John. (personal communication to Eastern Michigan University graduate art students, October 8, 1997).

98. Frye, Northrop. *Selected Poetry & Prose of William Blake*. New York: The Modern Library by Random House, 1953. "The Marriage of Heaven & Hell: Proverbs of Hell," p. 125.

103. Geldzahler, Henry. "Interview With Helen Frankenthaler." *Artforum* October 1965: pp. 36–38.

109. Williamson, Marianne, *A Return To Love*. New York: HarperCollins Publishers, 1992. p. 162.

124. Teresa, Mother, *A Simple Path*. New York: Ballantine Books, 1995. p. 93.

125. Wiseman, Carter. *I. M. Pei: A Profile in American Architecture*. New York: Harry N. Abrams, 1990. p. 90.

127. Chopra, Deepak. *The Path to Love*. New York: Harmony Books, 1997. pp. 4 & 33.

128. Emerson, Ralph Waldo. *Essays and Essays: Second Series*. Ohio: Charles E. Merrill Publishing, 1969. p. 139.

128. Chopra, Deepak. *The Seven Spiritual Laws of Success*. California: Amber-Allen Publishing, 1994. p. 32.

130. Kübler-Ross, Elisabeth. *The Wheel of Life*. New York: Scribner, 1997. pp. 283–86.

130. _____. *On Life After Death*. California: Celestial Arts, 1991. p. 3.

134. Motherwell, Robert. "Beyond the Aesthetic" *Design* April 1946: pp. 38–39.

143. Thoreau, Henry David. *Walden and Civil Disobedience*. New York: W. W. Norton & Co., 1996. p. 61.

145. Lowe, Janet C. *Warren Buffett Speaks*. New York: John Wiley & Sons, 1997. pp. 88–94.

146. Shakespeare, William. *Hamlet*. (I. iii. 78).

146. Henri, Robert. *The Art Spirit*. New York: Harper & Row, Publishers, 1984. p. 15.

Other Books and Videotape by Robert Piepenburg

If you would like to purchase Robert Piepenburg's videotape: *A Visit With The Artist*, order autographed copies of his books *Treasures of the Creative Spirit* and *The Spirit of Clay* or receive information about arranging for workshops please write to: Robert Piepenburg, c/o Pebble Press Inc., 24723 Westmoreland, Farmington Hills, MI 48336-1963